STUDY GUIDE
TO ACCOMPANY
AMERICAN CINEMA/
AMERICAN CULTURE

Second Edition

by Ed Sikov, Ph.D.

Boston   Burr Ridge, IL   Dubuque, IA   Madison, WI   New York
San Francisco   St. Louis   Bangkok   Bogotá   Caracas   Kuala Lumpur
Lisbon   London   Madrid   Mexico City   Milan   Montreal   New Delhi
Santiago   Seoul   Singapore   Sydney   Taipei   Toronto

Higher Education

Study Guide to Accompany American Cinema/American Culture, Second Edition
Ed Sikov

Published by McGraw-Hill, an imprint of The McGraw-Hill Companies, Inc., 1221 Avenue of the Americas, New York, NY 10020. Copyright © The McGraw-Hill Companies, Inc., 2005. All rights reserved.

This book is printed on acid-free paper

1 2 3 4 5 6 7 8 9 0   DOC/DOC   0 9 8 7 6 5 4

ISBN 0-07-310287-3

For Ethan Scheuer

About the Author:

Ed Sikov is the author of *On Sunset Boulevard: The Life and Times of Billy Wilder*; *Mr. Strangelove: A Biography of Peter Sellers*; *Screwball: Hollywood's Madcap Romantic Comedies*; and *Laughing Hysterically: American Screen Comedies of the 1950s*. He has written for such publications as *Premiere*, *Connoisseur*, *Spy*, and *Film Quarterly*, and he has taught at Haverford College, Colorado College, and Columbia University.

CONTENTS

INTRODUCTION

AN OVERVIEW OF THE COURSE

From the early years of the 20th century to the present day, audiences have learned about America by watching Hollywood movies. American films are the stories we tell ourselves—and the world—about who we are. Everything from our tastes in fashion to our preconceptions about race and gender is reflected by Hollywood cinema. In fact, one could argue that American films are so compelling in their depiction of our national outlook that the images become all the more difficult to see clearly. In a way, we are so familiar with the movies that both their methods and their messages seem like second nature.

American Cinema/American Culture, Second Edition, a textbook for an introductory course in American film and culture, brings Hollywood into clearer analytical focus. An art form, an industry, and a system of representation and communication, American film is a complicated and profoundly influential element of American culture. The course will explore how Hollywood films work technically, artistically, and culturally to reinforce and challenge America's national self-image.

In certain ways, this is a language course—the language of the motion picture. You do not have to learn this language to enjoy Hollywood movies; the events taking place on screen have always been immediately accessible to you. With most Hollywood films it is usually easy to follow the plot and pick up something about the characters. But without learning the language, the richness of these films is lost.

What is a shot? What is cinematography? What is film noir? These are some of the elements of film language you will learn in this course. Through the course you will increase your understanding of how films work as art and how they convey meaning as cultural artifacts. You will learn about the invention of the motion picture camera, the rise of the studio system, and the production of popular genres like the Western, the comedy, and the combat film. Most important, you will learn to become a more active and critical viewer. This course will help you to question the images of America you see on the movie screen and to redefine your own relationship to those images.

COURSE OBJECTIVES

American Cinema/American Culture and its supplementary materials are designed to enable you:

- to gain a working knowledge of American film history, from the silent cinema to the present day;

- to develop your cinematic literacy—in other words, to teach you to recognize and use the basic technical and critical vocabulary of motion pictures;
- to understand how the technology of the cinema relates to film art;
- to see and understand the place of Hollywood film in American popular culture;
- to grasp a fundamental understanding of the economics of the film industry;
- to understand the role of genre in American film history, and recognize how some of the most popular genres express American social and cultural tensions;
- to develop a more sophisticated conception of "realism" as it relates to motion pictures;
- to question your own role as a passive spectator, and increase your ability to watch films actively and critically.

COURSE COMPONENTS

American Cinema/American Culture provides a comprehensive introduction to American film and culture. The course consists of the following components, designed to be used either separately or in coordination with one other:

- the textbook *American Cinema/American Culture*, by John Belton, published by McGraw-Hill;
- *American Cinema*—ten one-hour television programs produced as a telecourse;
- three half-hour supplementary television programs;
- this study guide;
- optional supplementary films, to be assigned by the instructor or viewed independently by the student.

The Textbook

American Cinema/American Culture, by John Belton, is an independent textbook on American film history as well as a supplement to the thirteen programs in the telecourse. Many of the book's chapters parallel the television programs, and if you are using the telecourse, your instructor may assign reading strictly on that basis. But the book's function is more critical, for instead of simply repeating and expanding information contained in the television programs, the textbook explores many concepts on its own. From detailed historical and technical data to in-depth explorations of issues in film theory, the ideas explored in the textbook provide a comprehensive introduction to the field of film history and criticism.

The Television Programs

The ten one-hour television programs and three half-hour supplementary programs explore a variety of topics central to American film history, including the organization of the studio system, the nature of the Hollywood star, and the aesthetics and sociology of genres such as the Western and the film noir. Because these programs convey information about the art of the motion picture, they are integral educational tools for the telecourse. But unlike other telecourse programs in fields like biology or literature, *American Cinema* practices what it preaches: this telecourse is *itself* a part of the American cinema—a documentary film series about American films. In other words, you are invited to consider these programs *as films*. The critical vocabulary you learn *in* the telecourse will enable you to understand the filmmaking techniques used by the telecourse.

The Study Guide

This study guide supplements the textbook, links the textbook to the telecourse, and provides a key to learning. In all but one case, the units in this book correspond directly to the telecourse programs and provide a way to coordinate these programs with the textbook; an additional unit has been added on the musical, a topic for which there is no telecourse program. These study units will prepare you for reading the textbook chapters and, if you are using the telecourse, viewing the individual programs. They will also help you to evaluate and develop what you view and read by reinforcing key concepts and themes.

This guide is not a substitute for assigned textbook reading, nor does it provide a quick summary of the programs. It is instead a sort of tutor in book form—a means of organizing disparate information into a coherent learning experience.

This may be your first film course. If so, this study guide will steer you through the process of confronting an artistic medium with which you are already familiar but which you have never studied before. After all, we're presenting you with an entirely different way of watching movies—not as a passive spectator, but as an active student. As a result, the wealth of new information—the critical vocabulary used in the textbook, the hundreds of film clips seen in the programs—may be confusing to you at first. This book will help you to make sense of it.

The study guide contains eleven main units and three additional units, which accompany the aspects of film studies that can be taught throughout the course at the instructor's discretion. Each main unit of the study guide includes these sections:

I. **Overview**: a capsule discussion of the unit's central topic, with new terms appearing in italic type.

II.   **Screenings**: a list of films that pertain to the unit, noting those which are available on videotape and DVD; these films are optional elements of the telecourse (see the section on "Supplementary Films" below).

III.   **Study Plan for This Unit**
   • Getting Started: suggested ways of preparing for the class.
   • Watching: study tips for watching telecourse programs.
   • For Further Study: suggestions for retaining and developing the information conveyed in the program.

IV.   **Meet the Experts:** a short biographical guide to the people interviewed in the telecourse program.

V.   **Suggested Readings**: a short, annotated list of books and articles for further research.

VI.   **Exercises and Assignments:** a range of possible study tasks, designed to help you apply your learning to your own experience; these exercises are geared to a variety of educational settings and learning levels and appear in increasing order of difficulty.

VII.   **Self Test**: a short exam on the unit, designed to let you know how much you have learned.

The three supplementary units are designed to address specific technical, pedagogical, and theoretical topics of interest to an introductory class in film studies. The first is a survey of the formal language of Hollywood cinema, the second is a sample formal analysis, and the third is an overview of ideas about contemporary Hollywood filmmaking and film theory. These units do not contain suggested assignments and exercises, nor do they contain self tests.

An answer key to the exercises, assignments, and self tests will appear at the end of the book as Appendix 1. A glossary of film-related terms appears as Appendix 2.

Supplementary Films

American Cinema/American Culture and the *American Cinema* telecourse present a self-contained study of American film history. You will learn a great deal about the art of the motion picture just by reading the textbook and study guide and watching the programs. However, your instructor may wish to supplement the course by assigning individual films on videotape, DVD, or even 16mm prints. You will certainly benefit from viewing films independently regardless of course assignments.

Each unit of the study guide contains a list of suggested screenings—films that would be appropriate to each unit of the telecourse. Most of these films are widely available on videotape or DVD; check your college library, your local video store, or online for available titles.

Taking the American Cinema Telecourse

If you are taking the *American Cinema* telecourse for credit, you will need to find out the following information as soon as possible:

- how to register for the course;
- if and when an orientation session has been scheduled;
- if and when the *American Cinema* will be broadcast in your area, or where and when videotapes of the program will be screened;
- when course examinations are scheduled;
- if and when papers are due;
- if any additional on-campus sessions have been scheduled;
- if any supplementary screenings have been scheduled, and whether they are required or optional for the course.

To learn as much as possible from each unit, follow this general study plan:

1. Buy yourself a good notebook and label it for use only for this course.

2. Begin each unit by reading the study guide section, paying particular attention to the "Study Plan for This Unit" section.

3. Read the textbook chapters assigned by your instructor, or the suggested textbook reading assignment in the study guide. When you find a term or concept you don't understand, or if you read about an idea that you want to pursue in more detail, make a note of it in your notebook.

4. View the programs actively. This is a course on the mechanics of the movies. As you proceed through the course, you will acquire an increasing ability to watch films closely and see these mechanics at work. This ability requires concentration. If you find yourself slipping into the usual role of passive moviegoer, stop yourself. Take a few notes, or just stop and ask yourself what the images on the screen look like, then jot down a short description.

5. After watching the program, ask yourself if anything remains unclear, and reread those sections of the textbook and study guide.

6. Complete any assignments given to you by your instructor, or choose some from the "Exercises and Assignments" section of the study guide.

7. Keep up with the course. The *American Cinema* has been designed to provide a cumulative learning process; the concepts and terms you acquire in one unit will be used in future units.

8. Stay in close contact with your instructor. If he or she keeps regular office hours, stop by and introduce yourself if you haven't already had personal contact. If you are studying at a distance, keep in touch with your instructor by telephone. And don't be afraid to ask for individual

guidance. It's best not to wait until the final exam to discover all the things you could have asked but didn't.

9. This course is designed to change the way you see films. So, if you happen to go to the movies at any time during the course, by all means put what you have learned to use! Try to identify the filmmaking techniques used. Ask yourself if the film fits into any of the genres you are studying or whether the film reminds you of anything you have seen in the course. Gauge the extent to which you are learning to watch movies in a new way.

THE HOLLYWOOD STYLE

I. CLASSICAL HOLLYWOOD STYLE: AN OVERVIEW

What is Hollywood style? Everyone knows that Hollywood is a real place in Southern California, the heart of the American film industry. But Hollywood is also a powerful *idea*, the consequence of both a particular formal style of filmmaking and an industrial system of film production. This unit explores that style and system, their foundations in society and culture, and their joint economic and artistic evolution.

How is it possible for audiences who do not speak English to understand a Hollywood film? What makes Hollywood films similar to each other, no matter who directed them or when? What distinguishes them from one another? In what ways does a Hollywood movie have meanings that extend beyond its story? What makes an American film so smooth and seamless? And what makes that film so *American*?

These are broad, basic questions, but they raise some of the most critical issues in film history. To answer them, film historians have defined *classical Hollywood style* as a wide-ranging system of formal *conventions*, narrative devices, and industrial production techniques employed with extraordinary regularity in feature films made in the United States.

By *style*, historians mean the various elements of film art that produce expressive meaning: lighting, editing, set design, performance, dialogue, music, costume, and so on. As for *classical*, the word has traditionally referred to the way art forms like drama or sculpture conform to ancient Greek and Roman models. But to define Hollywood style as classical is to broaden the definition to include contemporary influence as well as historical origins. While certain elements of ancient drama can be seen in almost every Hollywood film (the rising and falling action of the plot and the centrality of a hero or heroine to the story, to cite only two), the American cinema is said to be classical because it has defined itself as *the* model of fiction filmmaking, the standard which all others must either imitate or oppose. Because of its undeniable success at storytelling, not to mention its domination of international markets, Hollywood films have produced the most influential set of filmmaking rules in the world. As a result, Hollywood style is as classical in its way as any of the great Greek dramas.

To understand classical Hollywood style, consider first the question of authorship. Who makes Hollywood films? In other art forms like painting or literature, the question of authorship seems simpler. Who painted the ceiling of the Sistine Chapel? Michelangelo. Who wrote *Pride and Prejudice*? Jane Austen. Although the act of individual creation is not in doubt in these instances, sophisticated discussions of the creative origins of works of art generally include questions of society as well. Art historians understand the Sistine Chapel's creation as a two-step process: the Italian Renaissance produced Michelangelo, and Michelangelo produced the Sistine Chapel's ceiling. Similarly, the social and literary history of England provided Jane Austen with the artistic conventions and cultural sensibility she employed in writing *Pride and Prejudice*.

Still, for most people the history of art and literature is usually understood as a chronicle of individual artists making their marks upon the world. Hollywood filmmaking, on the other hand, is a collaborative art produced in an industrial setting. Can Hollywood films even have an author?

The American cinema provides an interesting challenge to traditional art and literary criticism in this regard. Seeing film history solely in terms of individuals' proper names begs certain key questions. If one asks who made *Citizen Kane*, the answer seems obvious: Orson Welles. But who made *Lady Scarface*, *Parachute Battalion*, *They Meet Again*, and *The Devil and Miss Jones*? You could find out who directed them in a book of film trivia, but their directors' names would not tell you very much. You would discover that all of the films, including *Citizen Kane*, were made by the same studio, RKO, in 1941. Does this mean, then, that RKO is the author of *Citizen Kane*? What about the ways in which these films resemble other films from 1941—films made by Paramount Pictures, M-G-M, or 20th Century-Fox? What about these films' similarities to films made in 1932, or 1957, or 1993? Is the director *always* the author? Is he or she the *only* author?

The concept of classical Hollywood style begins with the idea that American films bear different authorial signatures, each providing a particular kind of meaning. Sometimes, as in *Citizen Kane*, the director's signature is very clear: Orson Welles cowrote the film, directed it, and played the leading role. Welles is one of the American cinema's most brilliant *auteurs*, or film authors. Experiencing and understanding Welles's expressive vision is every bit as exciting as listening to the music of a great composer or seeing a Van Gogh painting. With most films, however—films like *Lady Scarface* or *Parachute Battalion*—the director's signature is not as interesting, and one looks instead to the formal and narrative conventions employed not only in these individual films but in practically every film produced in Hollywood. Hollywood is thus itself a kind of author—a governing voice that continues to produce a set of films that use the same artistic methods and strategies to express a surprisingly rich and complex worldview.

No Hollywood director, producer, studio, or star has ever been entirely free of these conventions, no matter how idiosyncratic these artists and companies may have been. Even the most individualistic Hollywood directors, from D. W. Griffith to Stanley Kubrick, Francis Coppola, and Martin Scorsese, employ the conventions of classical Hollywood style. Talented directors play with these conventions, challenge them, revise them, and embellish them, but the conventional *system* is so effective, so highly developed and expressive, that it constitutes a kind of cinematic language, a way of "writing" which Hollywood filmmakers have found to be unusually articulate and aesthetically pleasing.

What are these conventions? Supplementary Unit A: "Film Language" gives you a capsule introduction to the elements of filmmaking such as editing, camera movement, subject-camera distance, focal length, lighting, ambient sound, and so on. (As one of three "supplementary" units, that unit has been designed to be used at individual instructors' discretion, either as an introduction to the course or a conclusion to it. Even if you have not been assigned to read that unit yet, you might want to take a look at it now.) In addition, Chapter 3: "Classical Hollywood Cinema: Style" in *American Cinema/American Culture* offers a descriptive glossary of film terms and a review of the basic formal elements of the cinema.

For the sake of this introduction, the first element to notice is that films are made of individual *shots* which have been carefully edited together. Instead of placing a spectator in a fixed position, as in a theatrical production, the film camera enables viewers to feel as if they are moving right onto the "stage" and into the action. In a combat film, for instance, one shot might be taken from inside an American bunker; the next shot might be from the enemy's position outside. The spectator is thus presented with literally opposing visions of the same event.

This formal shifting in perspective might be jarring, if it weren't for the specific formal techniques of classical Hollywood style. In Hollywood, the goal has generally been to keep the spectator from noticing every *cut*, or transition from one shot to another. In other words, classical Hollywood style usually attempts to keep editing as invisible as possible. In the program, editor Dede Allen, who edited such films as *Bonnie and Clyde, Reds,* and *Little Big Man*, describes this technique as a way of bringing the audience smoothly and surreptitiously into the middle of the action—to place the viewer "within the *proscenium arch.*"

To see what Allen means, try to imagine what it would be like to watch a film if you experienced a shocking visual jolt every time one shot joined another. Your filmgoing experience would be very different. Given that the average feature film today contains 600 to 800 individual shots, such jarring editing would make it difficult for audiences to sink into films' stories. How could one even begin to believe what's happening onscreen—even if it takes place in another galaxy—if editing did not aim toward smooth transitions between shots?

Hollywood cinema strives for this sense of believability. More than any other national cinema, American films are famous for their seemingly invisible editing. Some national cinemas have at various times aimed for a different goal. Early Soviet cinema, for example, often tried to *maximize* the impact of editing with the goal of encouraging the spectator to notice how and why films were constructed and, from this unsettling experience, form a revolutionary new reality in the mind. But in Hollywood, an elaborate series of formal techniques and narrative devices was developed to discourage audience awareness of the formal means of filmmaking.

In addition, Hollywood's narrative focus has generally been on an individual character and his or her goals. Film historian David Bordwell describes Hollywood films as tending to be about a character who wants something desirable, who is initially kept by outside forces from getting what he or she wants, but who, through luck and determination, achieves the goal in the end. Not every film follows this pattern. As Bordwell goes on to say, some films are about characters who want what they *shouldn't* have. What links these plot models is a concentration on individuality. This *myth* of individual success or failure is part of a particularly American vision, a way of seeing one's relationship to the world that this country's artists have explored from James Fenimore Cooper through F. Scott Fitzgerald and on to present day authors like Norman Mailer, Alice Walker, Chuck Palahniuk, and Allan Gurganus.

But film is different. Perhaps even more than literature is able to do, classical Hollywood film style operates on a process of *identification,* as audiences are encouraged by subtle visual and aural techniques to identify closely with the central character. Sometimes, identification is strengthened by *point-of-view shots,* in which the camera's field of vision is meant to be understood as that of a specific character, leading the audience to see the world, however momentarily, through the character's eyes. This is relatively rare, however. More commonly, audiences are encouraged to put themselves in the characters' places in a less literal manner through emotional identification rather than physical placement. In ways both subtle and obvious, Hollywood films tend to encourage audiences to believe that the protagonist of the film is an idealized version of themselves; we are asked to relate their concerns to our own and temporarily ignore the differences between their fictional world and our real one.

The apparent seamlessness of Hollywood editing becomes even more important in this regard. By hiding the cuts, Hollywood not only keeps the audience's attention focused on the characters rather than on the film's construction but also enables the viewer to travel anywhere within a scene without noticing these shifts in position and angle. Identification is thus all the more effective, since it occurs without the audience realizing it.

Throughout this course, you will explore some of the different means through which you are encouraged to identify with fictional characters in Hollywood films, and some of the problematic issues that result from such identification. For instance, what does identification with the outlaw hero of a Western suggest? With a heroic combat soldier? With a battling husband and wife in a screwball comedy? In addition, you will study the industrial methods Hollywood studios used to mass-produce these films, and the way the film industry has responded stylistically and economically to changes in American society. But no matter what the topic of the individual unit, the overriding issue of the course is to define and understand classical Hollywood style—what it means and how it works.

Hollywood style tends to be invisible; that is its nature. This course will help you to see it.

II. SCREENINGS

Each study guide unit contains a list of films appropriate to the particular area of film study covered by the unit. The unit on Westerns will have a list of Westerns, the unit on comedy will have a list of comedies, and so on. Given the topic of this initial unit, however, the list of appropriate films must necessarily be very broad. Virtually *any* Hollywood film from any period may be analyzed in terms of classical Hollywood style. Feel free, then, to view any movie you choose—any genre, any period.

Remember, though, that this is a college-level course in American film history. Since you can use the tools offered in this course to analyze any film, why not pick a great one to start with? You might choose an early film which pioneered the use of classical Hollywood style, or a later film which refined and developed the style. In addition, consider the topics of subsequent units; the film you screen now may be of use to you later in the course. Finally, the program on classical Hollywood style concentrates on several films in particular—*Scarface* and *All About Eve*, to name two. The textbook analyzes such films as *The Gold Rush*, *Rear Window*, *Some Like It Hot*, *The Terminator*, and *Mulholland Drive*. These films would be particularly worthwhile to screen on your own.

> *All About Eve* (1950)
> *The Aviator* (2004)
> *Bonnie and Clyde* (1967)
> *Bringing Up Baby* (1938)
> *Broken Blossoms* (1919)
> *Catch Me If You Can* (2002)
> *Citizen Kane* (1941)
> *City Lights* (1931)
> *The Crowd* (1928)
> *Dinner at Eight* (1933)
> *Double Indemnity* (1944)
> *Fight Club* (1999)
> *The General* (1926)
> *Gentlemen Prefer Blondes* (1953)

The Godfather (1972)
The Gold Rush (1925)
Goodfellas (1990)
The Grapes of Wrath (1940)
To Have and Have Not (1944)
The Lady Eve (1941)
Morocco (1930)
Mr. Deeds Goes to Town (1936)
Mulholland Drive (2002)
Orphans of the Storm (1922)
Pulp Fiction (1994)
Psycho (1960)
Raging Bull (1980)
Rear Window (1954)
Rebel without a Cause (1955)
Scarface (1932)
The Searchers (1956)
Sherlock, Jr. (1924)
Some Like It Hot (1959)
Stagecoach (1939)
Sullivan's Travels (1942)
Sunset Boulevard (1950)
The Terminator (1984)
They Were Expendable (1945)
Trouble in Paradise (1932)
Vertigo (1958)
What Ever Happened to Baby Jane? (1962)
The Women (1939)

III. STUDY PLAN FOR THIS UNIT

Getting Started

1. Read Chapter 1: "The Emergence of the Cinema as an Institution," Chapter 2: "Classical Hollywood Cinema: Narration," and Chapter 3: "Classical Hollywood Cinema: Style," in *American Cinema/American Culture*. If possible, read Supplementary Unit A: "Film Language" in this study guide.

2. Watch at least one of the films listed above, most of which are available on videotape or DVD. Here are some suggestions for selecting films:

   a) Most video stores and libraries have reference guides that provide short descriptions of films. Selecting a title at random may lead you to a film you might otherwise have ignored, but it can also lead you to a film you're not really interested in seeing. Analyzing films shouldn't be an empty exercise; take a few minutes to find a movie you think you'll like.

   b) Think about your own interests outside of this class. If you are interested in military history, try a World War II film such as *They Were Expendable*. If you like to read murder mysteries, try an Alfred Hitchcock suspense film like *Vertigo* or *Rear Window*.

   c) You may have seen one or more of these films already. It is always easy to say, "I've already seen that one," and leave it at that. But this course is designed to teach you to see films in a new way. Don't rely on your memory of a film you saw a few years ago, or even a few weeks ago. Get a fresh perspective.

   d) The textbook analyzes David Lynch's *Mulholland Drive* (2002) in great detail, so a fresh, recent viewing might be helpful.

3. As you watch the film you have selected, jot down any ideas or impressions you have. Don't worry if these ideas aren't worked out clearly; there will be time for that later. For now, just make a note of scenes or characters that strike your interest.

   a) Write a very short description of the main characters—who they are, how they act. Do they have identifiable goals? Do you relate to and/or identify with them?

   b) On the most basic level, does the film have what you think of as a "happy" ending, or is it more complex?

Watching

1. If you are utilizing the telecourse programs, take general notes about one or more of the central ideas raised in the program, such as:
   - the major formal elements of Hollywood style;
   - what *identification* means;
   - what seamless editing is and the implications of such editing;
   - the influence of classical Hollywood style on world cinema;
   - the nature of heroism in the gangster film *Scarface*.

   Take notes with an eye toward *ideas* rather than simple facts. And your notes don't have to be long and involved. They should be long enough and clear enough to jog your memory when it comes time to use your notes toward completing an exercise or writing a paper.

2. If one of these topics strikes you as particularly interesting, it might serve as the subject for a paper. More detailed note taking on this subject would be worthwhile.

3. As with the entire *American Cinema* telecourse series, the program offers many clips from different films. It will be impossible for you to remember all of these clips, or even to keep these clips straight in your notes. You will not be expected to memorize these clips, nor to describe them in great detail later. Instead, the clips are designed to give you both the flavor of individual films and an accurate overview of film history. The trick is to learn to use film clips to their best advantage—first, to begin to see stylistic patterns at work, and second, to see the clips as signposts that lead you to a richer experience of the films themselves.

As you watch the program, if you see a particular clip that grabs your attention, jot down the title and a simple description of the scene in a few words. For example: "*Scarface*—'the world is yours.'" Later on, you can view this film and do some additional reading about it.

For Further Study

1. Before too much time elapses after reading the textbook and/or viewing the program, fill in any gaps in your notes.

2. Ask yourself the following questions:
   - In what way were my expectations about Hollywood style confirmed? Did the textbook and/or program teach me what I already knew?
   - In what way were my expectations challenged? What did I learn? (Did you already know, for example, about the so-called 180-degree rule?)
   - Are there any issues that I would like to pursue further? (If not, don't be alarmed; the section "Exercises and Assignments" will suggest some ideas.) If an idea has already struck you as interesting, write it down now. With the program fresh in your mind, remember the points it raises and note as many as possible on paper. Keeping a record of what you are learning will help you to judge whether this course is worthwhile.

IV. MEET THE EXPERTS

Dede Allen is one of Hollywood's top film editors; her credits include *Bonnie and Clyde*, *Little Big Man*, *Dog Day Afternoon*, and *Reds*.

David Bordwell, a professor of film at the University of Wisconsin at Madison, is the author of *The Films of Carl-Theodor Dreyer*, *Narration in the Fiction Film*, and *Ozu and the Poetics of Cinema*; he also coauthored *The Classical Hollywood Cinema* and *Film Art: An Introduction*.

Allen Daviau is a cinematographer whose photography of *E.T.*, *The Color Purple*, *Empire of the Sun*, and *Bugsy* earned him Oscar nominations.

Lawrence Kasdan wrote and directed *Body Heat*, cowrote and directed *The Big Chill*, *The Accidental Tourist*, and *Grand Canyon*, and wrote the screenplay for *Raiders of the Lost Ark*, among other films.

Joseph Mankiewicz is the Oscar-winning director of *All About Eve* and *A Letter to Three Wives*; he also directed *Guys and Dolls*, *Suddenly Last Summer*, *Cleopatra*, and many other films.

Sidney Pollack has directed over 15 feature films, including *They Shoot Horses, Don't They?*; *Jeremiah Johnson*; *Tootsie*; *Out of Africa*; and *The Way We Were*.

Martin Scorsese is the director of *Mean Streets*, *Taxi Driver*, *The King of Comedy*, *The Last Temptation of Christ*, *Goodfellas*, *Cape Fear*, *The Age of Innocence*, *Gangs of New York*, and *The Aviator*, among other films.

Richard Sylbert is the production designer of such films as *Chinatown*, *Reds*, *Dick Tracy*, *The Cotton Club*, *The Graduate*, and *Rosemary's Baby*.

Bertrand Tavernier began his film career as a film critic and publicist; he cowrote and directed *Coup de Torchon*, *A Sunday in the Country*, *'Round Midnight*, and *Daddy Nostalgia*, among other films.

Robert Towne wrote the screenplays for *Chinatown* and *Shampoo*, among other films; he wrote and directed *Personal Best* and *Tequila Sunrise*.

V. SUGGESTED READINGS

Bordwell, David. "Classical Hollywood Cinema: Narrational Principles and Procedures," in Philip Rosen, ed., *Narrative, Apparatus, Ideology*, New York: Columbia University Press, 1986. A concise theoretical overview of classical style in Hollywood.

Bordwell, David, Janet Staiger, and Kristin Thompson. *The Classical Hollywood Cinema*. New York: Columbia University Press, 1985. Parts 1, 4, 6, and 7 treat various aspects of classical Hollywood style, including its historical development and the relationship between style and technology.

VI. EXERCISES AND ASSIGNMENTS

Throughout this study guide, the suggested activities contained in the "Exercises and Assignments" section have been designed for a wide variety of academic settings. Some are geared toward in-depth film aesthetics and analysis; they require access to videotapes or DVDs and the requisite video equipment. Others explore issues of history, sociology, and cultural studies and require access to standard research materials found in libraries. Still others focus on story and journal writing; these exercises require only pen, paper, and an imagination.

Here as elsewhere, they are arranged in increasing order of difficulty; in addition, the assignments as a whole will tend to become more challenging as the course progresses. Obviously, you will be tempted to do the first assignment in every unit and forget the rest. But ask yourself: What do I want to get out of this course? Choose an assignment that challenges you. If the first assignment is a genuine challenge, that's fine. By the end of the course, you will be able to tackle more difficult ones.

1. Make a list of everything you associate with the word "Hollywood." In other words, if someone described a film they had recently seen as "very Hollywood," what would you think about it? Would your sense of "Hollywood" change if that person was describing a movie from the 1930s rather than a current film? If so, how? This may seem like an extremely easy assignment, but if you put some thought and effort into it, it will show you the wide-ranging influence Hollywood has had on your experience of the world.

2. Many foreign filmmakers and American independent filmmakers have described the influence Hollywood has had on their own careers, even if they went on to make films that do not seem like Hollywood movies. For instance, Federico Fellini has said that he was influenced by Groucho Marx, and Spike Lee has described the ways in which he sees himself working in opposition to classical Hollywood. As a library research project, choose a foreign or American independent filmmaker whose work you have seen or about whom you would like to learn more, and try to find an interview or critical article that discusses Hollywood's influence on his or her work. If you are unfamiliar with library research, ask a librarian to help you.

3. Based on what you know so far about formal filmmaking techniques, construct a simple sequence that conveys the following information: a

crowd of people are watching a basketball game and one of the specta-tors is insane. *Construct the sequence using no more than three shots.* Do not worry about the sound track; this is a silent film. Remember, the camera can move anywhere you want it to move, but you may only use a maximum of three separate shots.

4. As both the textbook and the program have demonstrated, editing is one of the most important and meaningful formal elements in film. Analyze the editing of a film sequence of your choice. Begin by selecting a short but interesting sequence—the ending of *Scarface*, for example. Watch the sequence several times, if possible. Number each shot, and describe it in simple terms. (For instance, "The sequence begins with a low-angle shot of Tony Camonte at the top of the stairs, emerging from his hideout," and so on.) Once you have described each shot individu-ally, try to draw connections between them. What does each shot ex-press individually? What is expressed by editing them together?

VII. SELF TEST

1. Define or identify the following:
   (a) mise-en-scene
   (b) segmentation
   (c) *Citizen Kane*
   (d) Joseph Mankiewicz
   (e) three-point lighting
   (f) dramatic unities
   (g) modernism
   (h) seamless editing

2. Which of the following makes this statement false? The use of a zoom lens:
   (a) enables the camera to actually move from one place to another while always keeping the image in focus.
   (b) combined with a simultaneous tracking movement enabled Alfred Hitchcock to achieve a "vertigo effect" in the film *Vertigo*.
   (c) provides the impression of movement by shifting between wide-angle and telephoto focal lengths.
   (d) functions as a sort of consciousness surveying or studying the dra-matic action that takes place in its gaze, shifting perspective while remaining in one place.

3. Short answer: Describe the importance and effects of "matching" shots, noting the three main types of matches.

4. True or false:
   (a) A dissolve is a transition between two shots in which the first shot fades out while the second fades in.
   (b) Low-angle shots of a character generally tend to make that character seem diminished or inferior, though this is not always the case.
   (c) The formal technique known as the "iris-in" became popular in the early sound era, when improved technology enabled filmmakers to create new effects.
   (d) The so-called 180-degree rule says, in effect, that in order to maintain spatial relations within a sequence the camera must stay on one side of an imaginary line while the characters and other objects filmed must stay on the other.

5. Essay: What is classical Hollywood style? Describe its central formal and narrative features. Be thorough but concise.

THE STUDIO SYSTEM

I. THE STUDIO SYSTEM: AN OVERVIEW

From the 1910s and 1920s through the late 1940s and early 1950s, the American film industry organized itself around a relatively stable economic structure known as the studio system. Often condemned by critics for the lack of artistic independence it granted to filmmakers, the Hollywood studio system nevertheless provided a successful and efficient machinery for producing popular cinema. In fact, historically it has been the most coordinated, consistent, and commercially effective system of producing and distributing motion pictures in the world. Even those who attack the studio system for its inhospitality to certain directors must acknowledge that the system provided others with some sense of continuity and stability. For example, although Orson Welles did not work well under the studio system, George Cukor, Vincente Minnelli, Ernst Lubitsch, and Billy Wilder usually managed to do so.

The studio system is misleading in its very name. A studio is a room in which an artist creates his or her work, but Hollywood film studios were always much more complex in organization and operation. While these so-called studios—M-G-M, Paramount, Warner Bros., and others—did own the buildings and outdoor lots in which their films were shot, they also owned much more extensive and important properties: distribution companies, theater chains, even human talent through a system of exclusive long-term contracts. The complex industrial webs created by these film corporations, not the studio buildings themselves, are what made the system work with such extraordinary efficiency.

As you are learning in this course, Hollywood films may be analyzed in the same way one studies novels or paintings, but because the system that produces these works of art is an *industrial* phenomenon as well as an artistic one, Hollywood must be understood in economic as well as aesthetic terms. Specifically, classical Hollywood art is different from literature, drama, painting, and sculpture because it was produced through much the same industrial system that produced Ford cars, boxes of Wheaties, and bars of Ivory soap—in other words, *mass production*. And just as the American automobile industry has been dominated by a handful of corporations with well-known brand names, Hollywood in the studio era was run by a handful of powerful companies, each of which tried to put its own stamp of individuality on a field of similar products.

Five *major studios*, or *"majors,"* led the list—M-G-M (Metro-Goldwyn-Mayer), Paramount, Warner Bros., 20th Century-Fox, and RKO (Radio-Keith-Orpheum). These were followed by three *minor studios*, or *"minors"*—Columbia, Universal, and United Artists. A number of smaller *"poverty row"* companies brought up the rear—Monogram, Republic, Eagle-Lion, and others.

The majors attempted to model themselves on the factory system perfected by Ford and General Motors, but there were certain notable differences. On an automobile assembly line, each worker has his or her own specific task which he or she performs with the aim of creating a standardized product. Under the studio system, in contrast, a similar division of labor existed but the product—a movie—was unique in each instance. Every film had a producer, a director, a writer or two, and some actors, but it also had an art director, a set decorator, a staff of carpenters, a props person, a few electricians to set up the lights, a cinematographer, a camera operator, a costume designer, a wardrobe staff, an editor, and so on through the publicity staff and distribution executives. This immense industrial staff was employed to create *individualized* products, not mass produced cars or bars of soap. At the same time, all of these people were under contract to the studio to perform their tasks with a degree of regimentation that finds little parallel in any other art form.

The majors maintained a high measure of control over every aspect of film production and distribution through an industrial structure known as *vertical integration*. In the film industry, this term describes a film studio's ability to provide a film's financing, organize the talent necessary to make the film, supervise its filming and editing, and subsequently distribute it, publicize it, and in many cases even own the theaters in which it was screened. Even though the studio system was dismantled in the late 1940s, vertical integration is still at work today; Universal, for example, makes a film, distributes it, and books it into the Cineplex Odeon theaters which it owns.

One way to imagine the degree of control vertical integration afforded is to place yourself in the role of an independent filmmaker trying to compete with the studios. You have an idea for a film, but to organize the talent you must start from scratch, not only by writing the film yourself but by hiring each actor individually. Under the studio system, in contrast, screenwriters and actors were under long-term contract to the studio, so a pool of talent was always in place. As an independent filmmaker, you would need to search for outside financing unless you paid for the film yourself; the studios possessed the capital already. The studio owned vast tracks of land with *sound stages* and a huge outdoor *back lot* on which to create almost any fictional environment necessary; you, as an independent, need to rent facilities and build all the sets yourself. Finally, after much work, you have a finished film, fully edited and processed, "in the can." How are you going to distribute it? The majors had their own distribution network in place, not to mention their own chains of theaters, none of which would be available to you as an independent.

When one company achieves effective control over a given market, it is called a *monopoly*; when a group of companies achieves such control, it is known as an *oligopoly*. The majors constituted an oligopoly, and the control they exerted extended beyond their own vertically integrated operations. Although the studios owned theaters in some of the nation's most lucrative markets, they also assumed a high degree of control over other theater chains through practices known as *block booking* and *blind bidding*. Your textbook will describe these business tactics in greater detail, but in essence their effective consequence was to ensure that exhibitors were forced to show a whole string of a given studio's films rather than simply the most likely money-makers. As a hypothetical example, to get a high-budget Clark Gable film in the 1930s, theater owners had to agree to show three low-budget films with lesser stars. In this way, the studios ensured that *all* of their films had a market.

From the studios' point of view, the system worked very well. But beginning in the 1930s, the Justice Department began to attack the studio system on legal grounds. Using as a basis federal antitrust legislation that had been enacted to keep monopolies and oligopolies from preventing fair competition, the government launched a series of protracted judicial assaults on the studio system. Finally, in 1948, the Supreme Court decided in *United States v. Paramount Pictures, Inc., et al.* that the film industry's system of vertical integration did in fact constitute an illegal oligopoly, thereby forcing the studios to divest themselves of their theater chains. As a consequence of this decision and other sociocultural factors (the increasing popularity of television, shifts in leisure-time activities, and so on), the studio system ended. (You will learn more about the consequences of the studio system's collapse in Unit 9: "Hollywood in the Age of Television.")

Although the studio system was an industrial structure, its efficiency and longevity had artistic as well as economic effects. One of the recurrent questions posed by the studio system concerns the ability of studios to create their own individual styles. With their talent pools subject to long-term contracts, studios produced films that tended over the course of many years to be supervised by the same group of producers, written by writers under long-term contract, directed by a field of contracted directors, performed by a relatively stable set of actors, and designed by art directors and costumers who had worked under the same studio's roof for many years.

Is it possible, then, to perceive a studio's style? In the broadest terms, one may detect similarities among the films of a given company. One may also see certain contrasts from one studio to another. *American Cinema/American Culture* describes these stylistic tendencies in some detail. Paramount in the 1930s, for example, was known for its sophisticated, continental sensibility; this was largely because such émigré directors and art directors as Ernst Lubitsch, Billy Wilder, and Hans Dreier worked there. 20th Century-Fox, on the other hand, was known for a more homespun sensibility during this period with stars such Shirley Temple and Will Rogers. And M-G-M has always been characterized by the polish of its musicals and the glamour of stars such as Clark Gable and Greta Garbo.

But it is important to remember that these stylistic tendencies are only that—*tendencies*, not rules. Glossy, star-laden M-G-M, for example, produced Fritz Lang's *Fury* (1936), a film about mob violence, one of the bleakest and harshest motion pictures of its era. In addition, keep in mind that it is difficult to define studio styles accurately without seeing many, many films. The titles listed below in section II, "Screenings" have been selected to provide an array of characteristic styles. The studio system produced thousands and thousands of films, however, and each was unique.

II. SCREENINGS

Because this unit is, in part, about the ability of each major studio to create its own "studio style," the screenings list contains representative films by each of the five major and two minor studios during the height of the studio era. (As you will learn in the textbook, the third "minor," United Artists, was not really a film-producing studio but rather a distribution company for independently produced films.) You will get the general flavor of a given studio by seeing any one of these films. But if you have the time, see a few of them to compare one style to another. It's especially interesting to see how directors fared from one studio to another—Ernst Lubitsch at Paramount (*Trouble in Paradise*), at M-G-M (*The Merry Widow*), and at Fox (*Heaven Can Wait*); or John Ford at RKO (*The Informer*) and at Fox (*The Grapes of Wrath*).

Paramount:
  Duck Soup (1933)
  Easy Living (1937)
  The Lady Eve (1941)
  Morocco (1930)
  Trouble in Paradise (1932)

M-G-M:
  Dinner at Eight (1933)
  The Great Ziegfeld (1936)
  The Merry Widow (1934)
  Mutiny on the Bounty (1935)
  Queen Christina (1933)

RKO:
Cat People (1942)
The Hunchback of Notre Dame (1939)
The Informer (1935)
King Kong (1933)
Swing Time (1936)

20th Century-Fox:
Gentlemen's Agreement (1947)
The Grapes of Wrath (1940)
Heaven Can Wait (1943)
Little Miss Marker (1934)
Tobacco Road (1941)

Warner Bros.:
To Have and Have Not (1942)
I Am a Fugitive from a Chain Gang (1932)
Jezebel (1938)
Mildred Pierce (1945)
Public Enemy (1930)

Columbia:
The Awful Truth (1937)
Gilda (1946)
Golden Boy (1939)
It Happened One Night (1934)
Mr. Smith Goes to Washington (1939)

Universal:
All Quiet on the Western Front (1930)
The Black Cat (1934)
The Bride of Frankenstein (1935)
Imitation of Life (1934)
Shadow of a Doubt (1943)

III. STUDY PLAN FOR THIS UNIT

Getting Started

1. For a comprehensive view of the entire studio system, read Chapter 4: "The Studio System" in *American Cinema/American Culture*. The tele-course program, on the other hand, functions more as a case study of an

individual studio—Paramount Pictures. Reading the textbook first will place the program's treatment of Paramount in context.

2. Many of the study plans in this book will begin by suggesting that you watch a film. This unit is somewhat different from the others because it is mostly about business and economics rather than film style, a particular genre, or artistic trends in a given historical period. If you do wish to see a studio-era film to familiarize yourself with the kind of products the system produced, use the "Screenings" list above as a guide. If so, think ahead to subsequent units. Pick a comedy, for instance (*It Happened One Night*, *The Awful Truth*, or *The Lady Eve*) and get a head start on Unit 6.

3. If you screen a film, jot down any thoughts you have while watching it.

4. If you do not watch a film, simply ask yourself what your preconceptions of the studio system are. If you were asked what you know about how the old studio system differs from today's filmmaking environment, how would you respond?

Watching

1. If you watch the telecourse program, take some notes about main ideas raised in the program, such as:

   • how filmmaking under the studio system differs from contemporary Hollywood filmmaking;
   • the contrasting points of view about the studio system's value, both for art and commerce;
   • some ways in which Paramount's studio-era films are characterized stylistically and thematically;
   • the financial organization of the studios, and the influence of New York executives;
   • the relationship between the location of a studio's theaters to the films made by the studio.

2. Note the title and a brief description of any film clips that attract your interest. These clips may later serve as the basis for a research paper.

3. If you watch a film, jot down anything to comes to mind about *style* – the particular gloss of an M-G-M film, for example, or the grit of a Warner Bros. gangster film.

For Further Study

1. Fill in any gaps in your notes. You may very well have scrawled something quickly; you'll remember the point more clearly later if you flesh it out in detail now.

2. Ask yourself:
   - Did the program meet my expectations in terms of its content?
   - What did I learn that surprised me?
   - Did the program change the way I think about films from an earlier era?
   - Even at this early stage of the course, ideas may occur to you that might serve as a final paper topic. Write them down whenever you think of them, and if they strike you as especially good, mark them in some way that will attract your attention later. (These starred or underlined ideas will serve as some measure of what you have learned—even if they turn out to be not so good later!)

3. Think about the ways in which entertainment corporations influence your attitudes (not to mention your spending). Do you identify, say, the Walt Disney Co. with any particular *style* of film? How about video game companies? Do they have identifiable styles in what they produce? How would you describe these various styles?

IV. MEET THE EXPERTS

Peter Bart is the editor of *Variety*, the entertainment industry trade publication, and the author of *Fade Out: The Calamitous Final Days of M-G-M*; he was an executive for Paramount Pictures and M-G-M/UA.

Richard Brandt is president of the Translux theater chain; his father started the company in 1905, first as a chain of newsreel theaters and later as a chain of art cinemas.

Henry Bumstead has had a long and successful career as a Hollywood production designer; three of his notable films are *Topaz*, *Cape Fear*, and *Unforgiven*.

Edward Dmytryk began his Hollywood career as an editor, later moving into directing such films as *Murder My Sweet*, *Crossfire*, and *Raintree County*.

Michael Eisner served as head of production for Paramount Pictures before becoming chief executive officer at Disney.

Harrison Ford is the star of such films as *Witness*, *Blade Runner*, *Star Wars*, *Patriot Games*, and *Raiders of the Lost Ark*.

Douglas Gomery, a media historian and economist, is the author of *The Hollywood Studio System*, *Film History: Theory and Practice*, *Movie History: A Survey*, and *Shared Pleasures: A History of Movie Presentation*; he teaches at the University of Maryland.

Charlton Heston played Moses in *The Ten Commandments*, Michelangelo in *The Agony and the Ecstasy*, and the title role in *Ben-Hur*, as well as starring in such films as *Touch of Evil*, *Planet of the Apes*, and *Airport 1975*.

DeForest Kelley, best known for his role as Dr. Leonard "Bones" McCoy on *Star Trek*, was a Paramount contract player in the 1940s.

Howard W. Koch, Sr. began as an assistant editor at Fox and worked his way up to become head of production at Paramount in the 1960s.

Charles Lang is one of Hollywood's most brilliant cinematographers, having photographed such classics as *A Farewell to Arms*, *The Big Heat*, *Some Like It Hot*, and *Inside Daisy Clover*.

A. C. Lyles has worked continuously in various capacities at Paramount Pictures for over 50 years, having started as office boy for Adolph Zukor; he directed many Westerns in the 1960s.

Harold Michelson is a storyboard artist, responsible for planning the composition of shots before shooting begins; he has sketched storyboards for many filmmakers including Alfred Hitchcock.

Mace Neufeld is an independent producer whose credits include *The Omen*, *No Way Out*, *The Hunt for Red October*, and *Patriot Games*.

Phillip Noyce is the director of *Newsfront*, *Dead Calm*, *Patriot Games*, and *The Quiet American*.

Robert Parrish, who began his career as a child actor in *City Lights*, went on to become an editor for John Ford and later a director in his own right; he is the author of *Growing Up in Hollywood* and *Hollywood Doesn't Live Here Any More*.

Thomas Schatz teaches film history at the University of Texas at Austin; he is the author of *Hollywood Genres* and *The Genius of the System: Hollywood Filmmaking in the Studio Era*.

Catherine Turney, a staff screenwriter for Warner Bros. in the 1940s, wrote many scripts under sole credit—an unusual feat in the studio system, especially for a woman.

Meta Wilde has had a long and successful career as a Hollywood script supervisor since the 1930s, working mainly at Warner Bros.

V. SUGGESTED READINGS

Bordwell, David, Janet Staiger, and Kristin Thompson. *The Classical Hollywood Cinema: Film Style and Mode of Production to 1960.* New York: Columbia University Press, 1985. Parts 2 and 5 treat the corporate structure of studio filmmaking.

Gomery, Douglas. *The Hollywood Studio System.* New York: St. Martin's Press, 1986. An economic history of the studios, tracing their early organization, yearly profits and losses, and most profitable films.

Gomery, Douglas. *Shared Pleasures: A History of Movie Presentation.* Madison: University of Wisconsin Press, 1992. A look at how and where people actually experienced movies.

Schatz, Thomas. *The Genius of the System: Hollywood Filmmaking in the Studio Era.* New York: Pantheon, 1988. A detailed survey of the studio system, period by period, studio by studio, combining economic and stylistic analyses.

VI. EXERCISES AND ASSIGNMENTS

1. Using the textbook's description of a studio's various departments as a guide, diagram on paper the corporate structure of an imaginary Hollywood studio during the studio era. Compose it as a sort of family tree, with individual departments as branches and particular workers as leaves. How these departments and workers interact with each other will determine the shape of the tree. Keep in mind that studios not only made films but distributed and publicized them as well. How do these departments connect with the artistic departments? Who is at the top of the tree? Who is at the bottom?

2. Trace the progress of an imaginary film through the studio system from inspiration to exhibition. Be your own producer: steer the project through the system. Imagine the role each department would play in the production of the film. Cast the film yourself, using either imaginary or real actors. (This is an imaginary film, so don't be afraid to mix real stars from different time periods; cast Halle Berry alongside James Dean or Uma Thurman opposite Humphrey Bogart.) Develop a publicity campaign for your film, complete with advertising slogans, and imagine how the film would be released. Who is your audience? An urban crowd or people from small towns? Young people or middle-aged adults? Finally, decide for yourself whether your film would be a hit or a bomb, and explain why. To make the assignment function as a quiz, do not use the textbook as an open-book guide but instead try to re-

member the complexity of the studio system from your reading. (Note: you may either treat this as a straight assignment by describing the studio system soberly and accurately, or you may turn it into a satire of the studio system by coming up with ridiculous though revealing details.)

3. Certain directors' works appear and reappear throughout this course, both in the programs and in the textbook—John Ford, Howard Hawks, Preston Sturges, Frank Capra, and Billy Wilder are some of the most prominent. As a library research project, pick one of these filmmakers and trace his career through the various studios in which he worked. Ford would be an especially good choice, for his film style is classical (Unit 1), he worked successfully under the studio system (Unit 2) and made films with major stars (Unit 3). Ford did make a comedy or two (Unit 6), but he is better known for his Westerns (Unit 4) and combat films (Unit 7). In addition, he continued making films into the television age (Unit 9), and his influence can be seen in the work of certain younger directors (Units 10 and 11). In this way, your research project will provide important background information that will be useful throughout the course.

4. The question of studio authorship is one of the trickiest questions posed by Hollywood filmmaking. As an exercise in film theory, write an essay on the issue of authorship under the studio system. What evidence supports the notion of studio style? What makes the concept difficult to support? Can a given film bear more than one authorial signature? If so, how can they be distinguished? (Note: if you are familiar with any of the studio styles described in *American Cinema/American Culture*, use your knowledge as supporting evidence. If you are not familiar with these styles, draw instead on the resources you already possess: the factual information presented in the textbook and your previous experience with other art forms, not to mention reason and logic.)

VII. SELF TEST

1. Define or identify the following:
   (a) oligopoly
   (b) vertical integration
   (c) story department
   (d) block booking
   (e) RKO
   (f) *United States v. Paramount Pictures, Inc., et al.*
   (g) blind bidding
   (h) "minors"

2. Which of the following makes this statement false? 20th Century-Fox:
   (a) was known for its sophisticated, continental comedies.
   (b) was jokingly called "16th Century-Fox" because it continued to operate using outmoded business practices long after the other studios had abandoned them.
   (c) launched the career of Shirley Temple.
   (d) was headed for many years by Darryl Zanuck, known for developing the market for socially conscious films like *Gentlemen's Agreement* and *The Grapes of Wrath*.

3. Short answer: Name one reason why the studio system ended, and explain why.

4. True or false:
   (a) The studio system drew upon the techniques of mass production despite the fact that their product was a "nondurable" good.
   (b) Warner Bros. tended to market its films to an urban, working-class audience who favored gangster films and topical dramas seemingly ripped from newspaper headlines.
   (c) Originally, films were sold to exhibitors by the foot, like sausage.
   (d) Although the "majors" owned only a small percentage of the nation's movie theaters, the theaters they did own were so lucrative that they generated most of the nation's box-office receipts.

5. Essay: Did the studio system help or hinder American film art? (Note: there is no right or wrong answer here. The goal is to develop an argument and back it up with as many specific details as you can. You may find that the studio system both helped *and* hindered American film.)

THE STAR

I. THE STAR: AN OVERVIEW

In *Sunset Boulevard*, Billy Wilder's bitterly comic portrait of Hollywood stardom, Norma Desmond—a demented has-been movie star from the silent era—gazes distractedly into the air after shooting a screenwriter in the back and says, to nobody in particular, "The stars are ageless, aren't they? That's what makes one a star!" She raises a good question. Are stars ageless, or do audiences simply *want* to believe that they transcend time and other mortal boundaries? And exactly *what* makes one a star? Is it "star quality?" Acting talent? Good cheekbones? Hype? Are *all* film actors stars? What is the difference between an actor and a star?

The widespread impression that stars are somehow better than average people forms the basis of many fans' obsessions with individual performers. On the other hand, the slick, star-generating media machinery that bombards us with pictures of stars, gossip about stars, and a steady stream of product endorsements may provoke a critical backlash. How aesthetically important can movie stars be in this crass commercial context? If actors are like cattle, as Alfred Hitchcock once claimed, then perhaps stars are merely the prize-winning bulls and heifers in the barnyard of American culture.

In fact, stars are a very important element of American film aesthetics. They are also crucial to the economics of the motion picture industry. Stars and star images convey a wealth of connotations to an extraordinary number of people. The names John Wayne or Marilyn Monroe are, alone, enough to trigger a whole array of meaningful information all over the world. Stars' faces and physiques are as important to the films in which they appear as the faces and bodies depicted in any painting or sculpture. After all, they are often the most important objects on the screen, as central to film art as the face in a Rembrandt portrait or the body of Michelangelo's *David*. And unlike stars of the stage, movie stars can be seen in close-up, making the process of *identification* between audience and star all the more powerful.

As a product of American business, stars are powerful marketing tools. Every nation has its stars, but because of their economic clout, American stars may be the most consistently lucrative images in the world. As the textbook points out, the most famous face in the world belongs to a movie star—Mickey Mouse. The sheer amount of money generated by these images is itself enough to justify the academic study of stars.

To analyze the role and meaning of stars in the American cinema, critics have borrowed a term once used to describe the masks worn in Greek theater: *persona*. It's the root of the word "person," and the connection between the two is significant. In Greek theater, actors donned masks to differentiate various roles. In Latin, these masks were known as *personae*, and as the English language evolved, the word *person* came to be used to describe an individual human being. The etymology of the word *person* cuts to the heart of the problem as far as analyzing stars is concerned. Is a star an individual, a *person*, or is he or she an assumed role, a *persona*?

The answer is both. For example, John Wayne was obviously a real person—a college football player who appeared as a screen cowboy in the 1930s and then became world famous in the 1940s and 1950s when he performed in more expensive, commercially successful films. But he was also a persona—an image of self-confident masculinity, individualism, political conservatism, and American patriotism. In other words, John Wayne's persona reflected larger cultural concerns. Wayne's persona as an actor was built upon his film performances and was continually reinforced with each new film he appeared in, but his star persona was more overreaching than a simple list of film credits might suggest. As John Belton puts it, "A star is an actor whose persona transcends the sum total of his or her performances."

By appearing in a variety of roles over the course of many years, many actors develop personae. But not every actor becomes a star. A star's persona is different than an actor's persona. One way of understanding this difference is to look at Hollywood's *character actors*. As you now know, under the studio system actors were often signed to long-term contracts. As a result, each studio developed a stable of actors who would be cast in minor roles in film after film. Audiences would see, for instance, the same hefty, matronly woman over and over, often in the role of a down-home wife from the Midwest. They would see the same fussy, mustached man usually playing a shopkeeper, and the same round-faced Englishman turning up regularly as somebody's butler. These actors are known as character actors, and they each developed a specific screen persona—a mask they donned from one film to the next.

But these actors were not stars. A star's persona is a *second* mask partly covering the first. This secondary mask is not created solely on film but rather in the wider world of mass culture—in magazines, newspapers, advertisements, greeting cards, and so on. Look, for instance, at James Dean, an actor who played the leading role in *only three films*. The nature of these leading roles established his actor's persona—that of a rebellious, sexually magnetic youth who was attractive to both men and women. But his stardom was achieved through the mass reproduction of images of a leather-jacketed Dean on a motorcycle or in a sports car. These images, appearing regularly in the media, blended elements of Dean's real life with elements of his performances, but they were also meaningful in and of themselves because they reflected certain social desires and fears of the mid-1950s—ideas about American youth, male beauty, and contemporary anxiety. What cemented James Dean's stardom, however, was his early death when his Porsche sped out of control in the California desert. Like Jim Morrison, Dean's stardom was strongly enhanced by a strangely romantic death at a young age; Dean's persona as a rebellious youth was intensified because, in death, his image necessarily became eternally fixed in his early twenties. (Imagine, in contrast, an elderly James Dean holding his grandchildren on his lap, or a James Dean who had been killed after being run over by a laundry truck. His star persona would not likely have assumed the same dimensions.)

Stars reflect the needs, fears, and aspirations of American culture; our stars make sense to international audiences as embodiments of these concerns. And as American cultural needs shift, so do the types of men and women who become stars. *Maintaining* stardom across time therefore becomes difficult, especially during periods of social change. This is one reason why the popular notion of "star quality" becomes nearly impossible to accept. For instance, Theda Bara was one of the most popular stars of the silent era. She was physically appealing and performed well enough on screen, but would her so-called star quality work on films today? Not likely. Thus, explanations for stardom based on an actor's "charisma" do not begin to describe the mixture of conscious taste and unconscious ideology, reasonable talent and unreasonable hype, calculated career decisions and capricious turns of fate that make stars rise and fall from public favor.

Beginning in the silent era and continuing full force today, the American film industry has recognized its economic dependence on stars. Since every film is an unproven commodity, stars provide continuity in the marketplace, not to mention countless dollars worth of free publicity as stars' comings and goings are chronicled in newspapers and magazines and on television. For this reason, stardom—individual stars' careers as well as the whole star system—has been nurtured and sustained by way of a complex network of professional publicists and advertisers who are paid to dispense a constant flow of information about stars and the lives they are said to lead. Even in the case of relatively reclusive stars like Greta Garbo or Robert Redford, publicists are paid to manage personal information, in these cases by withholding it. These stars' public reticence only enhances their remote, larger-than-life personas.

In the studio era, studios often gave stars fake biographies to cover up unpleasant personal details. In addition, publicity photos were regularly airbrushed to enhance and further develop the idealized images they already projected onto movie screens. Today, most stars have personal publicists and thus do not need to acquiesce to studios' dictatorial publicity methods. And plastic surgery has taken the place of airbrushing—a less temporary mask designed, like make-up and camera filters, to idealize the human form.

What has not changed, however, is the nature of stardom, the wealth of cultural meaning projected from stars' onscreen and offscreen images. One may look at a star's individual performances, her or his career as a whole, and the publicity that helps to sustain her or his popularity, and see not simply an individual human being and an actor's mask but a mirror of our society. To answer Norma Desmond's question, then: stars express aspects of the culture that produced them, from the aesthetic quality of their photographed faces to the questions of gender, politics, psychology, and sociology raised by the popularity of their images. *That's* what makes them stars.

II. SCREENINGS

Since one of the stars on whom the telecourse program focuses is Joan Crawford, a number of Crawford's films are listed below. Crawford is a particularly interesting star to analyze because, although she maintained her stardom over the course of 90 films, most of these films were not particularly worthwhile otherwise. In fact, many of her later films—*Straight-Jacket, I Saw What You Did, Trog,* and so on—are truly awful. Of course you may choose to get a laugh out of these camp classics—even serious film scholars are allowed to have fun—but for a more complete picture of her career and screen persona, try to see at least one of Crawford's better films from the selection below.

Many other stars are mentioned in the program and/or the textbook. Three of them—John Wayne, Marilyn Monroe, Charles Chaplin, and Tom Hanks—make especially good case studies; a selection of their films is also noted. Finally, listed below are a group of films which not only feature stars but also are themselves *about* the creation (or destruction) of a Hollywood star.

About Stars and Star images:
  Inside Daisy Clover (1965)
  Mommie Dearest (1981)
  Singin' in the Rain (1952)
  A Star Is Born (1954)
  A Star Is Born (1976)
  Sunset Boulevard (1950)

Joan Crawford:
  Autumn Leaves (1956)
  Grand Hotel (1931)
  Johnny Guitar (1954)
  Mildred Pierce (1945)
  Our Dancing Daughters (1927)
  Possessed (1931)
  Rain (1932)
  What Ever Happened to Baby Jane? (1962)

A Woman's Face (1941)
The Women (1939)

John Wayne:
The Alamo (1960)
Fort Apache (1948)
The Green Berets (1969)
The Man Who Shot Liberty Valance (1962)
Red River (1948)
Rio Bravo (1959)
Sands of Iwo Jima (1950)
The Searchers (1956)
The Shootist (1976)
Stagecoach (1939)
They Were Expendable (1945)

Marilyn Monroe:
Bus Stop (1956)
Gentlemen Prefer Blondes (1953)
The Misfits (1961)
Monkey Business (1952)
Niagara (1953)
The Seven Year Itch (1955)
Some Like It Hot (1959)

Charles Chaplin:
The Circus (1928)
City Lights (1931)
The Gold Rush (1925)
The Great Dictator (1940)
The Kid (1921)
Limelight (1952)
Modern Times (1936)
Monsieur Verdoux (1947)

Tom Hanks:
Apollo 13 (1995)
Big (1988)
Forrest Gump (1994)
Philadelphia (1993)
Saving Private Ryan (1998)
Sleepless in Seattle (1993)
Splash (1984)

III. STUDY PLAN FOR THIS UNIT

Getting Started

1. Read Chapter 5: "The Star System," in *American Cinema/American Culture.*

2. Consider a simple question: who are your favorite stars and why do you like them? Don't just think about it; write your responses down in note form. Having answered the question simply, go a little further and ask yourself:
   - Do I find myself imagining that I would like these stars personally? If so, what do I really know about their personalities? How did I learn this information?
   - Can I explain what makes these people popular? What attracts me to them? What attracts others? Does race or ethnicity have anything to do with it?
   - What *cultural* information have I been given through my susceptibility to various stars? For instance, what have I learned about how women should or should not behave from a certain female star? How have my ideas about masculinity been affected by any male stars? Do I compare myself favorably or unfavorably to, say, Brad Pitt or Julia Roberts? How do I feel about that?

3. To begin to see the various elements of a star's construction and the cultural meanings his or her image conveys, screen at least one of the films listed above. As you watch the film, note the way you respond to the star—not the *character* he or she plays, but the *star*. What, if anything, does his or her image suggest to you? Is it possible to perceive any difference between the person and the persona while you are immersed in the film?

Watching

1. As you watch the film you choose and/or the telecourse program, take some notes about main ideas. In the case of a film, write down anything at all that strikes you; in the case of the telecourse, note, for instance:
   - the rise of the star system;
   - the relationship between film technology and stardom;
   - the ways in which the public's desire for stars is developed and encouraged;
   - Joan Crawford as a person and as a persona;
   - the nature of star performances within a film and from film to film;
   - the rise of Method acting in the 1950s.

2. Note the title and a brief description of any film clips that attract your interest. These clips may later serve as the basis for a research paper.

For Further Study

1. Go over your notes and fill in any gaps.

2. What aspects of the program do you disagree with? Did any of the experts make claims that you found suspect, incomplete, or downright wrong? Make a note of your responses. Bring up these questions with your instructor, or think about writing a short paper which attempts to prove the expert incorrect.

3. Take another look at your list of favorite stars. Have your responses changed in any way as the result of the program?
   - Have your assumptions about stars and stardom been challenged by the textbook and/or the program? Have you changed the way you think about movie stars?
   - What questions might you pursue in greater detail? Write them down in your notebook. If you are assigned a research paper or class presentation, you will have a head start in selecting a topic.

IV. MEET THE EXPERTS

Stella Adler, who studied acting under Konstantin Stanislavsky (who developed Method acting) has coached such stars as Marlon Brando, Robert De Niro, and Warren Beatty.

Ted Allan spent many years as a studio photographer for M-G-M, where he photographed such stars as Clark Gable and Jean Harlow.

Jeanine Basinger teaches at Wesleyan University; she is the author of *The World War II Combat Film: Anatomy of a Genre* and *The It's a Wonderful Life Book*.

Douglas Fairbanks, Jr. starred in such films as *The Thief of Bagdad*, *Gunga Din*, and *The Young in Heart*.

Danny Glover has starred in such films as *Places in the Heart*, *Witness*, *Grand Canyon*, and the *Lethal Weapon* series.

Sidney Guilaroff is a longtime studio hair stylist.

Jack Lemmon is the Oscar-winning star of such films as *Some Like It Hot*, *The Apartment*, *Days of Wine and Roses*, and *Missing*.

Ray Liotta has appeared in such films as *Field of Dreams*, *Dominick and Eugene*, and *Goodfellas*.

Ray London has worked as an acting coach for performers such as Geena Davis and Michele Pfieffer.

Karl Malden performed in *A Streetcar Named Desire*, *Baby Doll*, *On the Waterfront*, the television series *The Streets of San Francisco*, and countless American Express commercials.

Harry Mastrogeorge is an acting teacher.

Rick Nicita was head of the motion picture division of the Hollywood talent agency CAA, negotiating contracts and helping to shape the careers of Al Pacino, Francis Coppola, Oliver Stone, Ray Liotta, and others.

Julia Roberts has starred in such films as *Pretty Woman*, *Erin Brockovich*, *Ocean's Eleven*, *Steel Magnolias*, *My Best Friend's Wedding*, and many other films.

Henry Rogers is a longtime Hollywood publicist who helped build the career of Rita Hayworth, among other stars.

Jane Russell became a star because of (or despite) her role in Howard Hughes's notorious *The Outlaw*; she subsequently starred in *Gentlemen Prefer Blondes*, *The Revolt of Mamie Stover*, and other films.

Eva Marie Saint starred in Alfred Hitchcock's *North by Northwest*, Elia Kazan's *On the Waterfront*, and the television series *Moonlighting*.

William Tuttle is a former head of the make-up department for M-G-M.

Sylvia Wallace wrote about such stars as Joan Crawford and Cary Grant for the fan magazine *Modern Screen*.

John Waters is the director of *Multiple Maniacs*, *Pink Flamingos*, *Female Trouble*, *Polyester*, *Pecker*, and *Hairspray*, among other films, and the author of *Shock Value* and *Crackpot*.

Arthur Wilde worked as a studio publicist for Warner Bros. and is now an independent publicist.

V. SUGGESTED READINGS

Dyer, Richard. *Heavenly Bodies: Film Stars and Society*. New York: St. Martin's Press, 1986. An in-depth treatment of three stars—Marilyn Monroe, Paul Robeson, and Judy Garland—and their relationship to society.

Dyer, Richard. *Stars*. London: British Film Institute, 1979. An annotated survey of theoretical approaches to stars, covering issues of character, type, ideology, and audience response.

Gledhill, Christine, ed. *Stardom: Industry of Desire*. New York: Routledge, 1991. Theoretical essays on the meanings of stars and star images, the industrial construction of stars, and the role of spectatorship in stars' ability to communicate different messages to various segments of a mass audience.

Haskell, Molly. *From Reverence to Rape: The Treatment of Women in the Movies*. New York: Penguin Books, 1974. A history of women's images in American films; many stars are analyzed in regard to their personae.

Naremore, James. *Acting in the Cinema*. Berkeley: University of California Press, 1988. A historical analysis of Hollywood acting in the context of wider theatrical traditions; specific sections are devoted to such stars as Lillian Gish, Marlon Brando, Charles Chaplin, Cary Grant, and others.

Weis, Elisabeth, ed. *The National Society of Film Critics on the Movie Star*. New York: Viking, 1981. A collection of short, articulate essays on over 70 individual stars as well as on the role stars play in film aesthetics.

VI. EXERCISES AND ASSIGNMENTS

1. Using a current star as a case study, describe in detail the three levels of identity—the real person, the actor's persona, and the star's persona—that comprise his or her stardom. Use magazine profiles of the star, advertisements, films, gossip items, or any other element or product of popular culture as supporting evidence. Clip pictures of the star and include them as part of your study. *Analyze* these photos: what impressions are they calculated to convey? Ask yourself *how* you know what you *think* you know about the real person. If you have seen the actor appear in several films, try to determine what similarities there are between his or her various roles. (If you are a distance learner without immediate access to this kind of printed material, try watching several editions of a Hollywood "news" show such as *Entertainment Tonight*; try to determine how these shows construct and use star images.) Finally, take a stab at explaining the star's popularity. What, if anything, does the star say about American culture? (Some likely candidates include Denzel Washington, Tom Cruise, Halle Berry, Johnny Depp, Julia Roberts, Nicole Kidman, Uma Thurman, Jackie Chan, Jim Carrey, Jennifer Lopez, Samuel L. Jackson, and Lucy Liu.)

2. Many parallels may be drawn between Marilyn Monroe, one of the great female film stars of the 1950s, and Madonna, who holds a legen-

dary position in the music world. In fact, Madonna has consciously in-vited these comparisons not only by wearing Monroe-like outfits and hairstyles on many occasions but specifically by designing and choreo-graphing her "Material Girl" music video to mirror Monroe's rendition of "Diamonds Are a Girl's Best Friend" in Howard Hawks's *Gentlemen Prefer Blondes*, one of the 1950s great musical comedies.

Compare and contrast these two musical numbers. (*Gentlemen Prefer Blondes* is available on DVD; "Material Girl" can be found on DVD as well.) How is the image of women presented in each? Why does Ma-donna compare herself to Monroe? What is the nature of Madonna's commentary on women and sexuality? How does it differ from Howard Hawks's and/or Monroe's? (Note: if you care to pursue this topic fur-ther, ask your librarian for help in finding critical essays on Monroe and Madonna, both of whom are of great interest to critics.)

3. As a research project, select one of the five stars whose films are listed above in section II, "Screenings," watch one of these films, and try to determine how the star was being sold to the public at the time of the film's release. For a more ambitious project, read a biography of the star, and incorporate your findings into your essay. For example, what did America think about John Wayne in the late 1940s when he starred in *Red River*? How did the film's publicity help develop his stardom? Use the film's ads (found in almost any newspaper), behind-the-scenes arti-cles or profiles (check the *Reader's Guide to Periodical Literature*), ads for any products Wayne may have endorsed (such ads often appeared in *Look*, *Life*, and the *Saturday Evening Post*), and so on. Did the film's di-rector have anything to say about Wayne at the time? Did Wayne's star persona have anything to say about American culture at the time? If so, what? (Note: beware of broad generalizations based on a small amount of evidence.)

4. To pursue the meaning and nature of stars on a more advanced level, read and report on one of the scholarly studies noted in "Suggested Readings," above. (Check your library for availability; an interlibrary loan system may give you access to these titles even if your own library does not have them.) These critical works offer a number of intriguing and sometimes difficult challenges to the way one ordinarily thinks about film stars. Summarizing the critic's argument(s) will provide a sufficient assignment, but if you are able to go further, feel free to take issue with them, not only in terms of their treatment of individual stars but of their theories of stardom in general.

VII. SELF TEST

1. Define or identify the following:
   (a) Theda Bara
   (b) Konstantin Stanislavsky
   (c) *Singin' in the Rain*
   (d) Alfred Hitchcock's example of a perfect star
   (e) *Mildred Pierce, Grand Hotel, Rain,* and *The Women*
   (f) persona
   (g) one of the three films starring James Dean
   (h) Elia Kazan

2. Which of the following makes this statement false? Female film stars of the 1920s:
   (a) were often Victorian types who maintained an aversion to alcohol, a sense of self-control, and a conservative morality.
   (b) often played rebellious, sexually liberated types who nevertheless tended to settle down in the end and get married.
   (c) included Theda Bara and Florence Lawrence.
   (d) included Greta Garbo and Clara Bow.

3. Short answer: Describe some of the ways in which technology affected the phenomenon of stardom.

4. True or false:
   (a) 20th Century-Fox tried to manufacture another Marilyn Monroe in the form of such actresses as Doris Day and Julie Andrews.
   (b) 20th Century-Fox tried to manufacture another Marilyn Monroe in the form of such actresses as Sheree North and Mamie Van Doren.
   (c) The term "blaxploitation" refers to Hollywood's tendency to pay African-American stars less than they pay white stars.
   (d) Today, a top star such as Jack Nicholson plays an important economic role in the film industry because his presence virtually guarantees that foreign exhibition deals will be made even before the film goes into production.

5. Essay: Who were the first movie stars, how did they become stars, and why?

THE WESTERN

I. THE WESTERN: AN OVERVIEW

When the American cinema's powerful narrative drive confronts the distilled vision of history known as "the West," the result is a particularly American form of mythology. The Western, the American myth *par excellence*, is an extraordinarily popular and enduring film *genre*. Beginning with Edwin S. Porter's *The Great Train Robbery* (1903), the American film industry has produced more than 7000 Westerns. *Stagecoach* (1939), *Red River* (1948), *Johnny Guitar* (1954), *The Searchers* (1956), *Once Upon a Time in the West* (1969), and *Unforgiven* (1992) are only a few of the great Western films.

Maybe more than any other film genre, the Western has had a profound influence on the way the world views the United States and its people. From saloon brawls to war paint, the Western's *conventions* are almost as familiar to foreign audiences as the histories of their own countries. To Americans, the collective vision of American history conveyed by the Western is second nature—so much so that it is practically unconscious. The appeal of the Western is not surprising, for the genre's overriding concern is not only an important question in world history—how the New World was settled—but a basic issue for any society: what happens when culture and nature clash?

Most Westerns reassert America's optimistic vision of its own expansion westward in the 19th century, the cross-continental migration based on a political idea called *Manifest Destiny*. This theory held that the North American continent belonged to the United States by a combination of divine right, practical need, and the assumed superiority of American democracy. But some Westerns challenge that optimism. The genre's racial and political tensions are often explicit. Moreover, because Westerns are so thoroughly rooted in history, critical views of the Western tend to have as much to do with positive and negative ideas about the settling of the real American West as with the style and narrative structure of the films. Only by exploring the Western's nature as myth may one appreciate its art and understand its evolution.

Hollywood's West is obviously a geography of the imagination, but so was the West of 19th-century American arts and letters. Historian Frederick Jackson Turner, writing about the end of the frontier in the 1890s, was concerned as much with the *image* of the West as with the real men and women who farmed, raised cattle, and built towns there. To say that the Western is mythic is therefore not to say that it is false, but rather that it is a powerful popular fantasy that expresses deep truths and still deeper wishes about who Americans are as a people.

Westerns span American film history, from its earliest days to the present, and some are more complex than others. *A pictures*, like *Stagecoach* and *Red River* are especially rich in meanings, but even the old shoot-em-up *B-picture* Westerns and *serials*, which formed the backbone of the genre in the 1930s (with titles such as *Robin Hood of Eldorado* and *Tumbling Tumbleweeds*) may contain intriguing cultural, historical, and even sexual tensions. From big-budget epics like *Duel in the Sun* to *Dances with Wolves*, 1930s serials to 1960s television series like *Bonanza* and *Gunsmoke*, to HBO's 2004 series *Deadwood*, the Western is an ongoing genre of American self-definition.

Being explicitly concerned with America's past, Westerns bring with them a substantial amount of rationalization. By attempting to represent an idealized past and still remain true enough to present-day ideas to succeed as mass entertainment, Westerns must constantly rewrite history. Such reinvention is often seen as being simple falsification, and indeed many aspects of Western films bear little resemblance to hard facts. For example, a large percentage of real Western cowboys were black and latino, yet in almost no Westerns do black and latino cowboys appear. But in a way, it is precisely the discrepancy between fact and fiction that has enabled the genre to achieve its long-standing popularity. The repetition and variation in the genre—the Western's compulsion to cover similar ground over and over—testify not simply to its popular appeal but more specifically to an appeal that can never be fully satisfied. In other words, if every Western really did resolve its conflicts adequately and believably—if the West's reality could be represented once and for all—there would be no reason to produce over 7000 versions of the story.

Westerns in their broadest form provide the kind of wish-fulfilling reassurance that needs to be asserted again and again, as though certain darker secrets might be exposed if there were a lull in the action. Consider the decisive moment in John Ford's *The Man Who Shot Liberty Valance*, in which a newspaper editor, faced with a devastating contradiction between truth and fiction, spells out an important Western credo: "When the legend becomes fact, print the legend." (And notice—while the fictional editor prints the legend, the filmmaker, Ford, exposes it. In this case, audiences see the fact beneath the fiction.)

This contrast between myth and reality pervades the genre. In terms of Native American history, for instance, the genre as a whole tends to reduce a long and bloody history of racism and deceit to a conventional chase sequence with whooping "Injuns" and overly skillful white riflemen, thereby blaming the actual victim by casting him in the role of savage villain. Yet this carefully tailored, overtly biased version of real human suffering was practically required in terms of mass entertainment, for anything more honest would be too painful for most white Americans to watch.

As a culture, we keep telling ourselves that the issues are simple—the savages attack the innocent settlers. But the story we tell is so fundamentally unconvincing that we have to keep telling it over and over again to keep ourselves from thinking about what really happened. In this context, it's important to note that some of the great Westerns are much more interesting on the subject of Native Americans than the genre is reputed to be. Films like John Ford's *The Searchers* and *Cheyenne Autumn*, Samuel Fuller's *Run of the Arrow*, and Arthur Penn's *Little Big Man* bring racist tensions out into the open. While they may not resolve the issues adequately, they are nevertheless more disturbing than others in their conclusions.

The conflict between nature and culture on the North American continent, so essential to the Western, was the subject of art and literature long before the invention of the cinema. The paintings and sculptures of Frederic Remington, the poetry of Walt Whitman, the stories of James Fenimore Cooper, and the essays of Ralph Waldo Emerson are all concerned with the effect of civilization on an apparently uncivilized landscape, and vice versa. Owing to motion picture photography's great skill at capturing the staggering expansiveness and visual drama of Western terrains, not to mention the cinema's unique ability to move human beings across those terrains, the Western film recreates the conflict between nature and culture in a particularly vivid way. The fact that the cinema's invention coincided more or less exactly with the closing of the frontier enabled this conflict to be played out on movie screens long after it ceased to exist in reality.

The vicarious thrill of taming the frontier, which lies at the heart of the Western, is not limited to onscreen action sequences with sharpshooting heroes. It is also a visual, aesthetic pleasure. The gorgeous Technicolor cinematography of some of the epic Westerns of the 1940s and 1950s—King Vidor's *Duel in the Sun*, Anthony Mann's *The Man from Laramie*, and John Ford's *The Searchers*, to name only a few—enables audiences to experience the sheer spectacle of the West in a fresh, if idealized, manner.

As America's image of itself changed through each decade of the 20th century, the Western evolved as well. The types of Western heroes and the emotional tenor of Western stories have shifted to reflect and reinforce changes in audiences' attitudes. One can see the evolution on a fairly broad level in the career of John Wayne. A key Western hero, Wayne began his long career in Republic Pictures' B Westerns of the 1930s, in which he tended to play virtuous, clean-living cowboys with hearts of gold. With John Ford's *Stagecoach*, which elevated the Western to A-picture status, Wayne's character took on a more ambiguous morality. A decade later, in Howard Hawks's *Red River*, Wayne played an obsessive tyrant. Still later, in Ford's *The Searchers*, his character goes out of his mind, and by the time of his final Western incarnation in Don Siegel's 1976 film *The Shootist*, Wayne's gun-slinging Western hero, adrift and alienated in a world of automobiles and dry cleaners, finally gets mowed down in his last shoot-out.

In a certain sense, the onscreen death of John Wayne marked a turning point in the Western. From that moment on, every new Western Hollywood produces must be a double look backward—an attempt to rewrite not only American history but the history of the Western film itself.

II. SCREENINGS

Because of the Western's longstanding popularity, and because almost all of the major Westerns are now available on videotape or DVD, there are a huge number of films from which to choose. The following list contains a selection of the major Westerns, plus some lesser-known films which challenge traditional notions of the genre.

Bad Company (1972)
The Ballad of Cable Hogue (1970)
The Ballad of Gregorio Cortez (1982)
Barbarosa (1982)
Bend of the River (1952)
The Big Sky (1952)
The Big Trail (1930)
Broken Arrow (1950)
Buffalo Bill and the Indians (1976)
Butch Cassidy and the Sundance Kid (1969)
Cheyenne Autumn (1964)
Dead Man (1995)
Deadwood (TV-2004)
Destry Rides Again (1939)
Duel in the Sun (1946)
Fistful of Dollars (1964)
Fort Apache (1948)
The Good, the Bad, and the Ugly (1966)
The Great Train Robbery (1903)
High Noon (1952)
High Plains Drifter (1973)
Johnny Guitar (1954)
The Life and Times of Judge Roy Bean (1972)
Little Big Man (1970)
Lone Star (1996)
Love Me Tender (1956)
The Magnificent Seven (1960)
The Man from Laramie (1955)
The Man Who Shot Liberty Valance (1960)
McCabe and Mrs. Miller (1971)

The Missing (2003)
My Darling Clementine (1946)
The Naked Spur (1953)
Once Upon a Time in the West (1969)
The Outlaw Josey Wales (1976)
Pat Garrett and Billy the Kid (1973)
Posse (1993)
Rancho Notorious (1952)
Red River (1948)
Ride the High Country (1962)
River of No Return (1954)
Run of the Arrow (1957)
The Searchers (1956)
Shane (1953)
She Wore a Yellow Ribbon (1949)
The Shootist (1976)
Stagecoach (1939)
The Stalking Moon (1969)
Three Godfathers (1949)
Ulzana's Raid (1972)
Unforgiven (1992)
Wagonmaster (1950)
The Wild Bunch (1969)
Winchester '73 (1950)

III. STUDY PLAN FOR THIS UNIT

Getting Started

1. Read Chapter 11: "The Making of the West," in *American Cinema/ American Culture.*

2. Find at least one of the Westerns listed above, many of which are available on DVD and/or videotape. When going through the list of films available at your video store or library, keep an eye open for directors or stars whose work you have seen already.

Watching

1. As you watch the Western you have selected, jot down any impressions you have. Be especially aware of things you did *not* expect to see and hear.
   - Write down a few words to describe any characters who do not conform to your expectations—unusually strong women characters, for example, or heroes who are demonstrably crazy.
   - Write a very short description of the main characters—who they are, how they act, what they attempt to achieve, and whether they succeed.
   - If there are any spectacular landscapes in the film, describe them in a few words. Notice how the director treats the West *visually*.

2. If you are watching the telecourse program, take general notes about one or more of the central ideas raised by the program, such as:
   - the notion of heroic individualism in the Western;
   - the influence of real history on the Western myth;
   - the expressive quality of Western landscapes;
   - psychological elements of the Western: issues of masculinity and femininity, for example;
   - the depiction of Native Americans.

3. If one of these topics strikes you as particularly interesting, it might serve as the subject for a paper. More detailed note taking on this subject would be worthwhile. The more you prepare a paper in advance, the better it's likely to be.

For Further Study

1. Before too much time elapses after viewing the film and/or the program, fill in any gaps in your notes. Make sure they're legible!

2. Ask yourself the following questions in regard to the textbook, the film you've seen, and the program you may have watched:
   - In what way were my expectations about Westerns fulfilled? Did the film look like any television Westerns I have seen?
   - In what way were my expectations challenged? Did I already know, for example, about the shift in the Western protagonist in the 1960s from the active, heroic, good-guy type to what the critic Richard Slotkin describes as a "killing machine"?
   - What aspects of the film seemed inventive or unusual? What seemed conventional? What, in fact, *were* the conventions?
   - Are there any issues that I would like to pursue further? If something has already struck you as interesting, write it down now. With the

program fresh in your mind, remember the points it raises and note as many as possible on paper so that later, when you begin to write about the Western, you'll have a ready-made guide from which to begin.

IV. MEET THE EXPERTS

Lindsay Anderson, the author of *About John Ford*, is a British filmmaker who directed *If . . ., Britannia Hospital, Oh, Lucky Man,* and *The Whales of August,* among other films.

Budd Boetticher directed a cycle of spare, no-frills Westerns in the 1950s, including *Seven Men from Now, Decision at Sundown, Ride Lonesome,* and *Comanche Station.*

Niven Busch wrote the scripts for *The Westerner* and *The Postman Always Rings Twice* and the novel on which *Duel in the Sun* was based.

Clint Eastwood starred in the 1950s television series *Rawhide*, the story of an epic cattle drive from Texas to Kansas. The series lasted seven seasons, yet he never made it to Kansas. Eastwood went on to direct the Westerns *High Plains Drifter, The Outlaw Josie Wales, Bronco Billy,* and *Unforgiven.*

Monte Hellman directed such films as *The Shooting, Ride in the Whirlwind,* and *Two-Lane Blacktop.*

Elmore Leonard is the author of *Glitz, Hombre, 3:10 to Yuma,* and other novels.

Thomas McGuane wrote the screenplay for *The Missouri Breaks* as well as *Ninety-Two in the Shade* and other novels.

Arthur Penn directed such films as *The Left-Handed Gun, Bonnie and Clyde,* and *The Missouri Breaks.*

Thomas Schatz teaches film history at the University of Texas at Austin; he is the author of *Hollywood Genres: Formulas, Filmmaking, and the Studio System* and *The Genius of the System.*

Henry Sheehan writes film criticism for the *Los Angeles Times* and *Film Comment.*

Richard Slotkin chairs the Department of American Studies at Wesleyan University; he is the author of *Regeneration through Violence: The Mythology of the American Frontier, 1600-1860* and *The Crater*, a novel about the Civil War.

John Sturges directed *Bad Day at Black Rock, Gunfight at the O.K. Corral,* and *The Magnificent Seven.*

Bertrand Tavernier, a former film critic, cowrote and directed *Coup de Torchon*, *A Sunday in the Country*, *'Round Midnight*, and *Daddy Nostalgia*, among other films.

Rudy Wurlitzer wrote the screenplays for *Two-Lane Blacktop* and *Pat Garrett and Billy the Kid*.

V. SUGGESTED READINGS

Buscombe, Edward, ed. *The BFI Companion to the Western*. London: Deutsch, 1988. An encyclopedic guide to the genre, providing a fine overview as well as a lot of specific information.

Cawelti, John. *The Six-Gun Mystique Sequel*. Bowling Green, Ohio: Bowling Green State University Popular Press, 1999. An update of a classic analysis of the genre.

Gallagher, Tag. "Shoot-Out at the Genre Corral: Problems in the 'Evolution' of the Western," in Barry Keith Grant, ed., *Film Genre Reader*. Austin: University of Texas Press, 1986. An essay attacking most of the major critical works on the Western.

Pye, Douglas. "The Western: (Genre and Movies)," in Barry Keith Grant, ed., *Film Genre Reader*. Austin: University of Texas Press, 1986. An essay blending art history, literary theory, and film criticism.

Schatz, Thomas. *Hollywood Genres: Formulas, Filmmaking, and the Studio System*. Philadelphia: Temple University Press, 1981. A survey of the major genres in American film, including the Western.

Wright, Will. *Sixguns and Society: A Structural Study of the Western*. Berkeley: University of California Press, 1975. A genre study based on the structuralist theories of Vladmir Propp.

VI. EXERCISES AND ASSIGNMENTS

1. As a journal-writing exercise, ask yourself about your own preconceptions about the American West—both the old West and the modern West—and write them in rough form. Don't worry about composing a formal essay; concentrate instead on listing ideas. (Later, if you wish, you can turn these ideas into a complete paper.) If you are an Easterner and have never been to the West, so much the better: what do you *imagine* the West is like? *Why*? Ask yourself where you acquired the ideas you have, and whether or not they are fair or accurate.

2. As you have read in the textbook and seen in the program, the Western genre is made up of a classical type (broadly characterized by such films as *Stagecoach*, in which the hero, maintaining some sense of virtue, helps to tame the wilderness by defeating the forces of lawlessness) and a revisionist type (also broadly characterized by such films as *The Good, the Bad, and the Ugly* or *The Outlaw Josey Wales* in which the hero may be a criminal himself or may become a criminal through the pursuit of blind vengeance). Write a basic Western scenario and supply it with two different endings, a classical type and a revisionist type.

3. Create your own Western sequence out of the following basic situation: Two men are having a confrontation which ends in violence.
   - First: decide who these characters are. What is their relationship to each other? Are they brothers? Father and son? Rancher and cowboy? Sheriff and outlaw? White bounty hunter and Native American tribal elder? Give them any identities you wish.
   - Next: create a setting for these characters. Where are they? What is the *mise-en-scene*? Does the scene occur inside or outside? If it is outside, describe how the landscape looks. Is it a dusty desert or a lush ranch? Does it take place in a town or in the wilderness? If it takes place in a town, describe the degree of civilization there: is it a new town or an established one? Each of these elements will help to define the emotional tone the scene will take.
   - What are the characters wearing? Do they dress like stock Western characters straight out of central casting, or are they wearing something unique?
   - What are they arguing about? First decide on a general theme—land, a woman, a horse, a gun—and then, once you have narrowed it down, begin to write some lines of dialogue about this topic.
   - How does the scene end? How does the violence express itself?
   - Extra credit: Design a simple sequence of shots for this narrative. Place the camera anywhere you'd like, move it whenever and wherever you want, and cut to another shot whenever you think it is appropriate. Or, if you decide to film the whole bit in a single take, note where the camera is placed at all times. (You can do anything you want with the camera because your film only exists on paper!)

4. (*a*) To see how complex a film may be in terms of the sheer amount of expressive information it provides, watch the opening sequence of a Western and describe it in detail. (Note: *The Searchers, Red River, The Man Who Shot Liberty Valance*, and *Once Upon a Time in the West* contain especially rich opening sequences.) Pick out as many filmic elements as you can: what the image contains, where the camera is, whether the camera moves and when, what the lighting looks like, what the characters say, and so on.

(b) From the details you gather in your description, write a two- to three-page paper about what the opening sequence means in terms of the overall film. Why does the film begin as it does? How do the first few shots of the film relate to the last few? What are the major themes in the film? Does the opening sequence set up these themes? If so, how?

VII. SELF TEST

1. Define or identify the following:
   (a) B picture
   (b) Manifest Destiny
   (c) *Stagecoach*
   (d) genre
   (e) Sam Peckinpah
   (f) Monument Valley
   (g) myth
   (h) spaghetti Westerns

2. Which of the following makes this statement false? The historical development of the Western film:
   (a) reflects the cultural concerns of the 20th century.
   (b) occurred long after the end of the actual frontier era.
   (c) can be traced back to the tales of James Fenimore Cooper.
   (d) bears some relation to the rising popularity of 1970s films like *Star Wars*.

3. Short answer: Briefly describe some of the conventional ways in which Native Americans have been depicted in the Western. What do these images *represent*?

4. True or false:

   (a) In the late 19th century, Frederick Jackson Turner wrote that the frontier era ended; at the same time, the cinema was born.
   (b) In the 1960s, certain Westerns were seen as metaphors for the Vietnam war specifically because of the way they depicted Native Americans' struggle for freedom against white oppression.
   (c) In the 1950s and 1960s, Westerns began to concentrate on dangerous anti-heroes instead of virtuous protagonists.
   (d) An Italian film director was responsible for developing Clint Eastwood's Western screen persona.

5. Essay: In the program, film historian Thomas Schatz declares, "the Western is always about regret and it's always about loss." Do you agree? Ask yourself what things may have been lost, and whether you see those things as worthy of regret. Try to construct your essay in the form of an *argument*; take a specific point of view and prove it with concrete examples drawn from history, films, and/or your own experience.

THE MUSICAL

I. THE MUSICAL: AN OVERVIEW

At first glance, few film genres demonstrate America's changing tastes better than the musical. During the musical's heyday in 1936, for example, Hollywood released a whole string of feature-length musicals, from *Anything Goes*, *Show Boat*, *Follow the Fleet*, *Swing Time*, and *The Great Ziegfeld*, all of which became classics, to such now-forgotten efforts as *Strike Me Pink* and *Rhythmitis*. In 2003, in contrast, the Hollywood feature-length musical was represented by *The Singing Detective*, the animated *The Jungle Book 2*, and not much else.

But has contemporary America really turned away from the musical? Hardly. The runaway commercial success of the Oscar-winning live-action musical *Chicago* and the animated satirical musical *South Park: Bigger, Longer & Uncut* prove that Americans are still attracted to the genre in its more-or-less classical form—a fictional narrative interspersed with singing and dancing. And music videos are such an everyday part of our culture that we forget that in certain ways they're mini-musicals; we now expect that most popular songs will be illustrated on video with elaborately staged, expensively produced visuals that express something more than the music can communicate on its own. This unit explores some of the reasons for the musical's continuing popularity, its various narrative and non-narrative strategies, and the emotional responses audiences are invited to experience when film and video characters suddenly burst into song.

The first thing to consider in regard to the musical is the idea of *realism*. When people say they don't like musicals, they often cite the genre's lack of realism as the reason. But how realistic is, say, *The Matrix* or *Kill Bill Vols. 1 and 2*? Clearly it's the *kind* of realism that's at issue, not realism per se. Is it simply that it's "unreal" to watch a hiker suddenly become so overcome with rapture that she sings out "the hills are alive!" (accompanied by a full orchestra cleverly hidden offscreen) as Julie Andrews does in *The Sound of Music*? Maybe. But do the same people object when hip-hop artists and teen idols do essentially the same thing in music videos? Is it "realistic" for *anyone* to walk down a street or sit up in bed and just start singing?

In *American Cinema/American Culture*, John Belton points out that realism in the musical (and in cinema as a whole, come to think of it) is a matter of degree. In a musical, when an orchestra begins to play and characters start to sing, the narrative's more or less "realistic" world—the real Alps in *The Sound of Music*, a cheap apartment in *Chicago*— suddenly breaks open, and audiences are hoisted from that setting or space into what Belton calls a different *register*. In key ways, this new register is a joyful and liberating one. The old rules of behavior no longer apply: people get to sing instead of talk, and sometimes dancers even show up and illustrate characters' enhanced emotions with dazzling choreography and fabulous costumes. What a great fantasy of freedom!

This shift in register from narrative to spectacle, from linear story to nonlinear display, sparks an emotional *lift*—a kind of ecstatic pleasure. As Belton notes, *ecstasy* (from the Greek *ekstasis*) means "standing outside of oneself." That's exactly what Roxie Hart (Renee Zellweger) does in *Chicago* in many of her musical numbers. The film's first song, "And All That Jazz," is performed in a nightclub by Velma (Catherine Zeta-Jones), so it doesn't require any transition from the real space of the narrative to the fantasy space of the spectacle. It's grounded in the "reality" of the story; Velma sings and dances because that's her job. But with Roxie's first number, "Funny Honey," there is a more pronounced shift in register because Roxie is not yet a nightclub star; there's no narrative reason for her to suddenly start singing. So the director, Rob Marshall, cuts from a close-up of Roxie in her "realistic" drab apartment to a mirror-image close-up of Roxie in her own fantasy spectacle—onstage, bathed in blue light, and wearing a chic outfit—and only then does she begin to sing. In this way, even though the song is a slow-moving, smoky love song, Roxie is "ecstatic"; she stands outside of herself in her own imagination by escaping into fantasy.

Transitions from one register to another do not have to occur spatially in the musical. "Our children are out of control!" Kyle's mom screeches into the microphone at the censorship rally she has organized in *South Park: Bigger, Longer & Uncut*, and she quickly proceeds to get so worked up with emotion that she can't help but burst into song—the Oscar-nominated "Blame Canada." This, too, represents a shift in register. Kyle's mom lifts herself into an ecstasy of outrage, and suddenly the rules of the narrative—characters talk in prose, for instance—give way. Now they sing in rhyme and move in choreographed precision in a dance routine that leads them in a matter of seconds from South Park Elementary School to Mount Rushmore, the Liberty Bell, and finally the Capitol in Washington, D.C.

Spike Jonze's music video for Fatboy Slim's "Weapon of Choice" provides a literal example of *lift*. A businessman (Christopher Walken) sits alone in a slick, glossy hotel lobby. He hears music coming from a small radio sitting on a laundry cart, begins moving his head with the beat, gets up and starts dancing through the empty hotel, and finally ends up diving over a railing and flying around the atrium. The rules of gravity no longer apply, thanks to the music. (Spike Jonze is also the director of the films *Being John Malkovich* and *Adaptation*.)

Like *The Wizard of Oz, The Sound of Music, My Fair Lady,* and many other classic American song and dance films, *Chicago* and *South Park: Bigger, Longer & Uncut* are *integrated musicals*, meaning that the musical numbers are seamlessly combined with the story. *Backstage musicals* like *42nd St., Singin' in the Rain,* and the more recent *Moulin Rouge* solve the problem of integrating songs with narrative by setting the story in the world of theater or film production; whether they're putting on a Broadway show, making a movie, or appearing in a 19th century Parisian revue, the characters in backstage musicals have a built-in motivation to sing and dance. But as *Moulin Rouge* proves, backstage musicals are not necessarily more "realistic" than other kinds of musicals; *Moulin Rouge* grounds itself in backstage conventions, but a more stylized film is difficult to imagine. As with any discussion of realism in the cinema, let alone reality itself, it's only a matter of degree.

This brief overview has only touched on a few of the key issues, films, and personalities associated with the American musical. In this unit you will learn about Arthur Freed's marvelous M-G-M musicals of the 1930s, '40s, and '50s; the great, elegant dance team of Fred Astaire and Ginger Rogers; and theories of the musical's ideological strategies. You'll see how the genre rose and fell and rose again in terms of its commercial success. And you'll begin to put some of the analytical tools you're learning in this course to practical use in some of the assignments suggested below.

II. SCREENINGS

An American in Paris (1951)
Bells Are Ringing (1960)
Cabaret (1972)
Chicago (2002)
Coal Miner's Daughter (1980)
Dancer in the Dark (2000)
42nd Street (1933)
The Girl Can't Help It (1956)
Gold Diggers of 1933 (1933)
Grease (1978)
Meet Me in St. Louis (1944)
Moulin Rouge (2001)
My Fair Lady (1964)
New York, New York (1977)
Oklahoma! (1955)
Pennies from Heaven (1981)
Show Boat (1936)
Singin' in the Rain (1952)
The Sound of Music (1965)

South Park: Bigger, Longer & Uncut (1999)
Swing Time (1936)
Top Hat (1935)
Victor/Victoria (1982)

III. STUDY PLAN FOR THIS UNIT

Getting Started

1. Spend some time thinking about your relationship with music in general. Ask yourself what kind of music you listen to and why. What do you feel when you listen to music? Does it transport you emotionally in any way? If you believe you don't like film musicals, ask yourself why.

2. Read Chapter 7: "The Musical" in *American Cinema/American Culture*, keeping your personal responses to music in mind. Think about audience expectations about the musical during different periods in film history.

3. Choose one of the films from the list above or from the "Select Filmography" section in the textbook. Pick something you haven't seen before.

Watching

1. Watch the musical you have selected, paying particular attention to its type. Is it a backstage musical? An integrated musical? An operetta? Stop the video (if you can) when an idea strikes you, and jot it down. Note elements of costume and set design that seem particularly suited to this particular genre.

2. There is no telecourse program for this unit, so use the time to see another movie!

For Further Study

1. Take a look at the notes you have written; can you read them? Fill in any gaps.

2. Ask yourself:
   - What was my impression of American musicals before beginning this unit?
   - Were my impressions confirmed or challenged by the textbook chapter? By my professor in class? By the films and videos I watched?

3. Search online for reviews or essays about the film you watched, and compare your responses to the film with those of professional critics and scholars. (Note: one source for reviews of most recent and many older films is www.rottentomatoes.com.)

IV. MEET THE EXPERTS

Note: There is no telecourse program for this unit, so there are no on-air experts. The following people have played a significant role in the production or criticism of film musicals as described in *American Cinema/American Culture* and this study guide:

Rick Altman, the author of *The American Film Musical*, teaches cinema and comparative literature at the University of Iowa.

Fred Astaire starred in such great musicals as *Top Hat, Swing Time, Funny Face*, and many others.

Richard Dyer is the author of *Stars, Now You See It: Historical Studies on Lesbian and Gay Film*, and *The Culture of Queers*.

Arthur Freed began his career as a vaudeville performer and went on to create such classics as *The Wizard of Oz, Meet Me In St. Louis*, and *An American in Paris*.

Judy Garland starred in *The Wizard of Oz, Meet Me in St. Louis, A Star is Born*, and many other films.

Gene Kelly choreographed and danced in such musicals as *An American in Paris, Singin' in the Rain, It's Always Fair Weather*, and *Brigadoon*.

Baz Luhrman directed *Moulin Rouge, Strictly Ballroom*, and *Romeo and Juliet*.

Rob Marshall directed Bob Fosse and Fred Ebb's musical *Chicago*.

RKO is the studio at which Fred Astaire and Ginger Rogers made their most famous musicals.

Martin Rubin, the author of *Showstoppers: Busby Berkeley and the Tradition of Spectacle*, is a film programmer at the Art Institute of Chicago.

Ginger Rogers starred in a number of musicals with Fred Astaire, such as *Flying Down to Rio, Roberta,* and *Top Hat.*

Matt Stone and Trey Parker created the great American musical *South Park: Bigger, Longer & Uncut.*

Warner Bros., despite its reputation for gritty gangster films in the 1930s, also produced such extraordinary musicals as Busby Berkeley's *Gold Diggers of 1933* and *42nd Street.*

V. SUGGESTED READINGS

Altman, Rick. *The American Film Musical*. Bloomington: Indiana University Press, 1987. An anthology of critical essays on the genre, together with an annotated bibliography by the film historian Jane Feuer.

Collins, James M. "The Musical," in *Handbook of American Film Genres*, ed. Wes D. Gehring. Westport: Greenwood Press, 1988. A concise survey of the genre.

Croce, Arlene. *The Fred Astaire & Ginger Rogers Book*. New York: Galahad Books, 1972. A critical look at America's most famous dance team by a noted dance critic.

Dyer, Richard. "Entertainment and Utopia," *Movie* 24 (Spring, 1977). A theory of the musical's ideological project(s) through the years.

Feuer, Jane. *The Hollywood Musical*. Bloomington: Indiana University Press, 1982. A short but wide-ranging primer on the genre, covering questions of audience identification, genre style, and ideology.

Rubin, Martin. *Showstoppers: Busby Berkeley and the Tradition of Spectacle*. New York: Columbia University Press, 1993. An analysis of Berkeley's elaborate stage and screen styles.

VI. EXERCISES AND ASSIGNMENTS

1. Watch a music video by your favorite recording artist, and try to put some of the ideas generated by this unit to critical use. In a sense, the entire video may provide the "lift" described in the textbook. Ask yourself why the video looks the way it does; why the performers act the way they do; and whether the video is "realistic" and why. Write your responses in rough form.

2. As an advanced project, find out who directed the video you have watched. Online resources will be very helpful. Has this person directed other videos you have seen, or any feature films? Is he or she known for having a particular visual style? Incorporate your findings with your personal response to the video and write a 3- to 4-page paper. Don't worry too much about fashioning a polished paper; just see where your ideas and feelings take you.

3. *Treatment* writing. In film, a treatment is an outline for a screenplay written in prose form. A good treatment tells the story in broad terms, describes the characters simply but clearly, and conveys the emotional tone of the film. Treatments may be as short as a page or two, although they may be longer for more complicated story ideas.

Write a treatment for a music video based on the song of your choice. Re-imagine the song's video if one already exists. Cast and style it the way *you* see it, not the way it has already been made. Describe the sets, props, and costumes you would like to see; map out action, including some choreography that expresses what *you* hear in the song. Create a story around the song the way you see and hear it; or, make it non-narrative as you see fit. Let your imagination take you wherever it wants. But do write your treatment on paper or type it on a computer rather than just thinking about it. Structure it, and put it into words. This will help clarify your ideas.

VII. SELF-TEST

1. Define or identify the following:
   (a) *Chicago*
   (b) Trey Parker
   (c) Gene Kelly
   (d) ekstasis
   (e) Queen Latifah
   (f) Busby Berkeley
   (g) Judy Garland
   (h) Arthur Freed

2. Which of the following make this statement false? Fred Astaire and Ginger Rogers:

   (a) were top musical stars of the 1960s.

   (b) appeared in musicals that were considered old-fashioned when they were made.

   (c) displaced their characters' sexual desire into fighting with each other.

   (d) made most of their films for the Walt Disney Company.

3. Short answer: What does the term "lift" mean in regard to film musicals?

4. True or false:

   (a) *The Jazz Singer* was the first movie musical.

   (b) Musicals of the 1960s such as *Mary Poppins* and *The Sound of Music* were box-office failures when they were released; audiences had grown tired of musicals.

   (c) Movie musicals are judged by the degree to which they are realistic; a musical that seems phony has failed in its goals.

   (d) *Moulin Rouge* was filmed entirely on location.

5. Essay: Write a 5-page essay about the music video of your choice. Describe its technical features (such as cutting and camera movements) using the terms you have learned in this course. Pursue your ideas in any direction you wish; use the following questions only as a guide. Can you describe the video as being in any way *realistic*? If so, what is the nature of its realism? Is there a narrative thread to the video, and if so, what story does it tell? Does the video alternate between two *registers*, as film musicals do? If not, how does the video operate instead? Do the musicians play a role in any narrative the video has, or are they in a world of their own—the realm of music? Does the content of the song have anything to do with the images presented? If not, why not?

AMERICAN COMEDY

I. AMERICAN COMEDY: AN OVERVIEW

From Charles Chaplin and Buster Keaton to John Belushi, Eddie Murphy, and Jim Carrey, American film comedy has given audiences the chance to give proper behavior a black eye in the name of laughter. Breaking rules can be dangerous in real life, not in film comedy. Onscreen, bad manners and non-conformism are not only permissible but laudable. Chaplin's Tramp character, for instance, enjoys kicking people in the rear end when he doesn't get his way—policemen's butts are a particularly inviting target. Keaton, a more intellectual *persona*, embraces a peculiar form of paranoid absurdism as a means of coping with a hostile world. Racing in panic from a bizarre mob of would-be brides in *Seven Chances*, or battling what seems like the entire Union Army in his Civil War comedy *The General*, Keaton embodies the kind of intense, modern anxiety that civilized customs simultaneously provoke and suppress. Watching Chaplin and Keaton outwit civilization is liberating, especially for those in the audience who cannot do it as successfully.

John Belushi's grossness, Eddie Murphy's street smarts, and even the self-defensive violence perpetrated by Macaulay Culkin in *Home Alone* give audiences similar vicarious pleasures. Screen comedians get to behave in ways the rest of us cannot, and we enjoy seeing normal rules of behavior explode. But there may be a catch. Having blown these social norms to bits, do comedies tend to glue them back together again at the end?

Both the telecourse program for this unit and this study guide chapter focus on romantic comedies, from the *screwball comedies* of the 1930s and 1940s to 1980s comedies like *Look Who's Talking* and *Desperately Seeking Susan*. The textbook takes a much broader perspective, since not all American comedies are romantic in nature. Chaplin, Keaton, and the Marx Brothers, for example, are not romantic comedians, and neither are John Belushi, Eddie Murphy, Bill Murray, Richard Pryor, or any of the actors and actresses who appear in the *Police Academy*, *Naked Gun*, and *Airplane* series. *Dumb and Dumber* is a great comedy, but it's not exactly romantic.

The romantic comedies on which the program focuses are some of the most sophisticated films in the American cinema, but it is important to keep in mind that comedy itself is fairly "vulgar" to the extent that it is aimed toward a very wide audience. In Latin, *vulgus* means "the common people." In ancient drama, tragedy concerned nobility; comedy was usually much lower, both in class and tone. Screwball comedies thus provide an interesting point of departure for studying comedy in general, for although they often center on the lives of the rich, they yank these lives down to a common level by subjecting them to ridicule.

The aim of screwball comedy is similar to the baseball pitch for which it was named. Screwball comedies take funny turns and spin in unexpected directions. In these films, love often begins to look a lot like hatred, and romance comes to resemble farce as some of the best looking, most elegant actors and actresses in Hollywood—Cary Grant, John Barrymore, Irene Dunne, Myrna Loy, Carole Lombard, and William Powell—appear in roles expressly designed to make them look like idiots.

Audiences at the time certainly appreciated screwball comedies. Some, like Frank Capra's *It Happened One Night*, were extremely successful at the box office; others, like Howard Hawks's *Bringing Up Baby*, were not. But regardless of their individual commercial appeal, at least 75 screwball comedies were made between 1934 and 1942, and they continue to be some of the most enjoyable and critically respected films in Hollywood history. *The Lady Eve*, *His Girl Friday*, *The Palm Beach Story*, *The Awful Truth*, and *Twentieth Century* are only a handful of the classic comedies produced in this period.

Many film critics have tended to understand screwball comedy as a reflection of the Great Depression. To support this claim, these critics cite the abundance of wealthy characters, often women, who fall in love with someone in a lower social class. In *It Happened One Night*, for instance, the heroine, an heiress, rejects her engagement to a flashy playboy, the toast of the upper class, in favor of a man-of-the-people journalist. According to these sociologically minded critics, even films which center exclusively on the foibles of the rich are meaningful in specifically economic terms, for these films are said to serve the cultural function of humanizing the wealthy in a time of widespread poverty and social unrest. Instead of making rich people seem villainous or culpable, Hollywood (which was, after all, run by wealthy studio bosses) made them seem merely crazy, quaint, and harmless—sillier versions of the common you and me to whom the films purportedly appeal. As the working-class heroine of *Fifth Avenue Girl* so succinctly puts it, "Rich people are just poor people with money."

There is much to be said for this sociological approach. Screwball comedies sometimes do perform a democratizing function. At times, they attempt to resolve class differences in the form of marriages between members of the upper and middle classes. (Marriages between rich and *poor*, however, are rare to the point of nonexistence.) In addition, they often push America's aristocracy off the twin pedestals of good taste and respectability by making them look stupid and childish. And there is no denying that almost all of these films were made during the Great Depression, which obviously influenced their social visions. For instance, when an heiress marries a newspaper reporter at the end of a Depression-era film, as in *It Happened One Night*, something is clearly being said about resolving class conflicts, albeit in an idealized way.

At the same time, screwball comedies operate on a more subversive cultural and psychological plane. To be blunt about it, most screwball comedies are more about sex than they are about the Great Depression. One way of understanding this aspect of screwball comedy is to chronicle some of the outrageous emotional and even physical cruelty couples administer to each other; warfare which generally has little to do with money problems or class issues.

For example, John Barrymore jabs a pin in Carole Lombard's butt in *Twentieth Century*. Rosalind Russell hurls her pocketbook at Cary Grant in *His Girl Friday*—and judging by his quick reaction it is not the first time it's happened. Carole Lombard slams the door in Robert Montgomery's face in *Mr. and Mrs. Smith*. ("Goodnight, dear," she says, "your nose is bleeding.") William Powell locks Myrna Loy in a closet in *After the Thin Man*. In a particularly harsh scene in *Nothing Sacred*, Fredric March punches Carole Lombard senseless. Henry Fonda locks Margaret Sullavan into a straitjacket in *The Moon's Our Home* and Claudette Colbert does the same to Gary Cooper in *Bluebeard's Eighth Wife*. Myrna Loy has her husband William Powell committed to an insane asylum in *Love Crazy*. Henry Fonda and Barbara Stanwyck slap each other in the face in *The Mad Miss Manton*. And in *Unfaithfully Yours*, one of the last screwball comedies made, Rex Harrison fantasizes about slitting Linda Darnell's throat with a straight razor. *These are all comedies.*

Why is there such hostility between people who are supposed to be in love? Without getting into the question of whether men and women are *ever* able to get along with each other—a question which has vexed comedy writers (not to mention psychotherapists) from Aeschylus through Shakespeare to present-day comedians such as Woody Allen and the writers and performers of "Northern Exposure"—it is necessary to look not at the Great Depression per se but some specific events of that era.

In Hollywood, one of the most important turning points of the 1930s was the institution of an enforceable *Production Code* in 1934. In the era of *There's Something About Mary*, it's hard to imagine severe restrictions on the content of Hollywood films, but in fact the Production Code was extremely restrictive. It was imposed precisely to curtail what the nation's moralists thought was the rising tide of immorality in Hollywood movies in the early 1930s. It is therefore no coincidence that 1934 was also the same year that witnessed the birth of the screwball comedy with such films as *It Happened One Night*, *Twentieth Century*, and *The Thin Man*. The result of more than a decade of protests by members of the clergy and conservative politicians, the Production Code forbade explicit sex, adultery, and homosexuality from the screen. Restrictions on the contents of comedy were only one aspect of the Code, but this aspect was crucial to the development of Hollywood comedy. As the Code put it flatly, adultery "is never the subject for comedy."

Unfortunately for the Code and its proponents, adultery and the threat of adultery, not to mention sexual confusion and violent jealousy, have *often* been the subjects of comedy throughout western culture—especially *romantic* comedy. For reasons that have less to do with economics than with human sexual relations, audiences have long found squabbling lovers to be very funny, either on stage or in the pages of books. Keeping sex out of romantic film comedy was therefore nearly impossible.

What the Code did, in spite of itself, was to force American comedy to take a new form. By preventing characters from engaging in sexually suggestive dialogue, let alone explicit onscreen sex, the Code succeeded in forcing comic characters to put their energies to a distorted end—bickering, screaming, and, whenever necessary, slapping and punching. Some screwball comedies resolve these tensions by establishing stability through a new social order; *It Happened One Night* is the classic example. Others may *seem* to affirm stability by way of a final marriage or kiss, but actually call such stability into question. For instance, heiress Katharine Hepburn and paleontologist Cary Grant finally stop fighting and hug each other at the end of *Bringing Up Baby*, but just at that moment the brontosaurus skeleton Grant has been laboriously constructing collapses into chaos.

Screwball comedies are fascinating for precisely this reason: the line between conflict and resolution is unusually blurry. Both comic conventions and the structures of classical Hollywood style mandate a so-called happy ending, the happiness in question being the institution (or reinstitution) of marriage. But in screwball comedies, happy endings often make even less sense than usual, given what we've seen earlier in the film. In *Unfaithfully Yours*, Rex Harrison, caught up in a violent jealous rage over his wife, sums up the spirit of screwball comedy when he describes the double feature he has just seen: "I saw a very long picture about a dog, the moral of which was that a dog is a man's best friend, and a companion feature which questioned the necessity of marriage for eight reels and then concluded it was essential in the ninth." In this regard, Hollywood's failure to resolve the conflicts it explores is itself the source of liberating laughter.

II. SCREENINGS

This screenings list is divided into four sections: screwball comedies, the films of Charles Chaplin, the films of Buster Keaton, and a group of comedies from the 1950s through the early 2000s. If you have the time, see more than one.

Screwball Comedies:
After the Thin Man (1936)
The Awful Truth (1937)
Ball of Fire (1942)
Bringing Up Baby (1938)
Easy Living (1937)

His Girl Friday (1940)
Holiday (1938)
I Was a Male War Bride (1948)
It Happened One Night (1934)
The Lady Eve (1941)
Love Crazy (1941)
Midnight (1939)
Monkey Business (1952)
Mr. and Mrs. Smith (1942)
Mr. Deeds Goes to Town (1936)
My Favorite Wife (1940)
My Man Godfrey (1936)
Nothing Sacred (1937)
The Palm Beach Story (1942)
The Philadelphia Story (1940)
The Thin Man (1934)
Twentieth Century (1934)
Unfaithfully Yours (1948)

Charles Chaplin:
The Circus (1928)
City Lights (1931)
The Gold Rush (1925)
The Great Dictator (1940)
The Kid (1921)
Limelight (1952)
Modern Times (1936)
Monsieur Verdoux (1947)

Buster Keaton:
The Cameraman (1928)
College (1927)
The General (1927)
Our Hospitality (1923)
Seven Chances (1925)
Sherlock, Jr. (1924)
Spite Marriage (1929)
Steamboat Bill, Jr. (1928)

Comedies from the 1950s to the early 2000s:
Annie Hall (1977)
Austin Powers: International Man of Mystery (1997)
Being John Malkovich (1999)
Blazing Saddles (1974)
Desperately Seeking Susan (1985)

Eternal Sunshine of the Spotless Mind (2004)
Fast Times at Ridgemont High (1982)
The Girl Can't Help It (1956)
Housesitter (1992)
Manhattan (1979)
Pillow Talk (1959)
Revenge of the Nerds (1984)
The Seven Year Itch (1955)
A Shot in the Dark (1964)
Some Like It Hot (1959)
South Park: Bigger, Longer & Uncut (1999)
There's Something About Mary (1998)
Victor/Victoria (1982)

III. STUDY PLAN FOR THIS UNIT

Getting Started

1. Read Chapter 8: "American Comedy," in *American Cinema/American Culture*.

2. The telecourse program you may be assigned deals with three broad types of American comedy: the screwball comedy, popular in the 1930s and 1940s; sexually complicated comedies of the 1950s, such as *Some Like It Hot*; and 1980s romantic comedies such as *Broadcast News* and *Look Who's Talking*. Try to see a film from one of these periods:

   (a) *It Happened One Night, His Girl Friday*, and *Some Like It Hot* are treated in depth in the program. These films would be especially appropriate selections.

   (b) If you are particularly interested in questions of gender, sexuality, and repression, try *Some Like It Hot, Seven Chances*, or *Victor/Victoria*.

   (c) Or, see a contemporary comedy such as *There's Something About Mary* and explore the differences between earlier periods and the present day.

Watching

1. Whatever film you choose, take general notes as you watch it, paying particular attention to the ways in which it may surprise you.

2. If you watch the telecourse program, note on paper the main ideas presented by the program, such as:
   - the relationship between screwball comedies and the Great Depression;
   - the role repression plays in screwball comedy—what is repressed, and how it may find expression in other forms;
   - the key character types in screwball comedy—heiresses, journalists, and others;
   - screwball comedy's conflicted view of love and marriage;
   - differing critical analyses of key screwball comedies such as *The Lady Eve* and *His Girl Friday*, their relationship to the genre and to society;
   - the social development of romantic comedy from the screwball era to the present day, especially in the treatment of women.
   - If any film clips spark your interest, write their titles down, together with a brief description and any pertinent quotations. You may want to use this information later in preparing an essay.

For Further Study

1. As always, fill in any gaps in your notes.

2. After reading the textbook, seeing a film, and/or watching the telecourse program, ask yourself:
   - Did I expect to learn what I did? Did this unit confirm what I thought I already knew?
   - How did the unit change my perceptions about film comedies?
   - Did the textbook and study guide authors' and telecourse talking heads' analyses of comedy in general and individual comedies in particular make sense to me? If so, am I able to outline some of them briefly? If your answer is no, it would be a good idea to write down the questions you have and ask your instructor, either during or after class.
   - Are there any issues that I could pursue in greater detail? Keep track of them in your notebook.

IV. MEET THE EXPERTS

Edward Bernds was the sound recordist for *It Happened One Night* and *Twentieth Century* as well as many other films.

Peter Bogdanovich directed the comedies *What's Up Doc?* and *Illegally Yours*, as well as such films as *The Last Picture Show*, *Mask*, and *Saint Jack*; he has also written works of film criticism, including monographs on Howard Hawks, Orson Welles, and Alfred Hitchcock. He appears on *The Sopranos* as Dr. Kupferberg.

James L. Brooks is the writer-producer-director of *Terms of Endearment* and *Broadcast News* and the creator of the television comedy series *The Mary Tyler Moore Show* and *Taxi*.

Nora Ephron wrote the screenplays for *Heartburn* (based on her novel), *Silkwood*, and *When Harry Met Sally*, and she directed *This Is My Life* and *Sleepless in Seattle*.

Molly Haskell, the author of *From Reverence to Rape: The Treatment of Women in the Movies*, has taught film history at Columbia University.

Amy Heckerling directed *Fast Times at Ridgemont High*, *Look Who's Talking*, *Look Who's Talking Too*, and *National Lampoon's European Vacation*.

Garry Marshall wrote and produced the television comedy series *The Dick Van Dyke Show* and *Happy Days*; he is the director of *Pretty Woman*, *The Flamingo Kid*, and *The Princess Diaries* among other films and television shows.

Thomas Schatz teaches film history at the University of Texas at Austin; he is the author of *Hollywood Genres* and *The Genius of the System: Hollywood Filmmaking in the Studio Era*.

Susan Seidelman directed *Desperately Seeking Susan*, *Smithereens*, *Making Mr. Right*, and *She-Devil*.

Ed Sikov is the author of *Screwball: Hollywood's Madcap Romantic Comedies*; *Laughing Hysterically: American Screen Comedies of the 1950s*; biographies of the director Billy Wilder and the comedian Peter Sellers; and this study guide.

Robert Zemeckis directed *Who Framed Roger Rabbit?*, *I Wanna Hold Your Hand*, *Romancing the Stone*, *Forrest Gump*, and the three *Back to the Future* films.

V. SUGGESTED READING

Cavell, Stanley. *Pursuits of Happiness: the Hollywood Comedy of Remarriage*. Cambridge: Harvard University Press, 1981. Philosophical and aesthetic readings of some of the great romantic comedies of the 1930s and 1940s, centering on Cavell's notion that these comedies resolve failed marriages by deepening couples' knowledge of themselves, each other, and the moral world around them.

Paul, William. *Laughing/Screaming*. New York: Columbia University Press, 1994. A theoretical and practical treatment of comic vulgarity, centering on the intersection of gross-out horror and comedy films of the 1970s and 1980s; includes a detailed reading of Chaplin's *City Lights*, centering on Chaplin's fondness for anal and phallic humor.

Sikov, Ed. *Screwball: Hollywood's Madcap Romantic Comedies*. New York: Crown, 1989. A critical and historical survey of screwball comedy focusing on comic hostility and the expression of repressed sexual energy and tensions.

Carney, Raymond. *American Vision: The Films of Frank Capra*. New York: Cambridge University Press, 1986. A critical survey of Capra's career; the material on *It Happened One Night* is especially relevant to this unit.

VI. EXERCISES AND ASSIGNMENTS

1. Develop two one-page scenarios—one comic and one noncomic—out of the following basic situation: a man and a woman are arguing about their apparently failing relationship. (The noncomic treatment may take the form of a murder mystery, a melodrama, or any other genre you choose.) The characters and at least *some* of what they say and do should be the same in both treatments. Describe the characters, provide some colorful details about the setting of the sequence, and compose a few lines of dialogue for each treatment. (Use the guidelines noted in Unit 4, Exercise 3.)

   When you have completed both treatments, write a two-paragraph explanation of *why* one is funny and the other is not. Become your own film critic: try to explain your artistic choices in terms of what you have learned about comedy.

2. Debates about film censorship, morality, and artistic freedom from which the Production Code arose have continued in various forms through the years. Write an essay on the question of whether Hollywood films should or should not have any restrictions imposed upon

them. Take any position you wish on this issue, but remember, you *must* base your opinions on historical and/or current events research. Find information on current guidelines on film content, for example. Who defines the difference between PG-13 and R? Are there any sociological studies that suggest that sex and violence in film have no effect on the behavior of the audience outside the theater? Are there studies that prove that such a relationship exists? Argue your case according to your own point of view, and be as opinionated as you like. But be sure to back up your opinions with facts.

3. Write a close analysis of a sequence from the film of your choice. You may approach this assignment in several ways. If you would like to do a visual analysis, begin by numbering each shot of the sequence and describing it in detail. Develop the analysis further by analyzing the formal relationships between shots; see if you are able to detect a pattern. Finally, try to discover what formal elements, if any, make the sequence comic. Another way of approaching the assignment is to do a narrative segmentation as described in Chapter 2 of the textbook. Break the film's story line into its essential elements, and describe the pattern that emerges. How does the film's conclusion relate to its beginning? What has changed? What has remained the same?

4. To pursue comedy from a theoretical perspective, read either Henri Bergson's essay "Laughter" or Sigmund Freud's *Jokes and Their Relation to the Unconscious*, both of which should be available in your college library. How do these theoreticians explain comedy? Write a 4-5 page essay summarizing the major points raised in either work, and support or refute the theories by citing examples from a film comedy. If you are able, draw in some of the critical opinions floated in the program. Ask yourself how well any of these theories explain your own experience of film comedy.

VII. SELF TEST

1. Define or identify the following:
   (a) the Tramp
   (b) *vulgus*
   (c) the democratizing function of American comedies
   (d) Frank Capra
   (e) Production Code
   (f) screwball comedy
   (g) *The Lady Eve*
   (h) Sigmund Freud

2. Which of the following makes this statement false? Screwball comedies:
   (a) began with the four Marx Brothers, whose characters engaged in both "low" slapstick and "high" romantic comedy.
   (b) inevitably end in happy marriages, thereby reaffirming the social order.
   (c) are, as one critic put it, sex comedies without the sex.
   (d) were brought into being by the Production Code, which was made enforceable and more restrictive in 1924.

3. Short answer: In broad terms, describe Buster Keaton's comic style and note some of his greatest films.

4. True or false:
   (a) Harold Lloyd's screen persona reflected the middle-class values of his era: status, optimism, and "making it" in the business world.
   (b) Although it is now considered a classic screwball comedy, *It Happened One Night* was a box-office bomb that was applauded only by a handful of film critics.
   (c) Unlike tragedy, comedy tends to celebrate the idea of social change.
   (d) Ethnic and racial humor was never common in Hollywood films until the Civil Rights movement paved the way for treating the issues openly.

5. Essay: Did the Great Depression affect American comedy? If so, how? If not, why not?

6. Extra credit: Name something gross that occurs in *There's Something About Mary*.

WAR AND CINEMA

I. WAR AND CINEMA: AN OVERVIEW

Before the Vietnam war, when graphic moving images of real combat were brought directly into American living rooms for the first time by way of television, most people in this century saw war through the eyes and cameras of Hollywood filmmakers. It almost goes without saying that war has a lengthy history in entertainment because long before cinema was invented men and women read combat tales such as Homer's *The Iliad* (the Trojan wars), Tolstoy's *War and Peace* (the Napoleonic wars), and Stephen Crane's *The Red Badge of Courage* (the American Civil War), to name only a tiny fraction of the combat narratives in literature. But in terms of *seeing* war, it was Hollywood that defined the visual and cultural parameters. Even after the Vietnam experience radically changed the way Americans look at war, Hollywood continues to shape our imagination of combat.

World War I tested the new cultural importance of the cinema by providing a rallying point for patriotism in films such as D. W. Griffith's *Hearts of the World*. In the following two decades, *pacifism* and *isolationism*—the historical results of that bloody and, to many people, inexplicable global disaster—were given wide popular expression through films such as King Vidor's *The Big Parade* and Lewis Milestone's *All Quiet on the Western Front*. But when World War II broke out in Europe and the Pacific, and the United States found itself needing to justify its participation to a frightened and confused populace, Hollywood took the opportunity to define not only the nature of the conflict but also the myth of who Americans are as a nation. In short, Hollywood explained what America was fighting for.

With those World War II combat films that were made during the war itself, Hollywood wrote the stories, chose the locations, cast the soldiers, and provided the special effects, all under the influence of the federal government's *Office of War Information*. At no other time in its history has the American entertainment industry been subjected to such overarching government control.

In its mix of politics and art, long-standing myth and immediate cultural need, the World War II combat film—those made during the war and those made after it—is one of the cinema's most fascinating and least appreciated genres. From these films one can gain a clear understanding of how American culture creates broad cultural myths; how they may be used to serve contemporary political goals; and how Americans saw themselves during the period in which the United States became a superpower. The Vietnam combat film offers a similar set of ideas and meanings, as do Gulf War films. These films are explicitly about power, conflict, and violence. In addition, watching a combat film can be a satisfying aesthetic experience. Like it or not, the spectacle of war, with all of its violence and inherent narrative tension, is an enduring aspect of almost every culture in the world. To be blunt, if war films weren't entertaining, nobody would watch them. Even a film as disturbing as *Schindler's List* made a profit.

If a film genre is a collection of shared conventions, a repetitive set of cultural rituals, what are the primary conventions of the war film? One key ritual is *demographic* in nature: the creation of an ideal American troop onscreen to resolve some problematic divisions offscreen. To an even greater extent than World War I, the Second World War threw together nonprofessional American soldiers from a wide variety of backgrounds. White farm boys from Mississippi found themselves sharing barracks with Polish-Americans from Chicago, Jews from Brooklyn, Italian-Americans from Boston, and Native Americans from Arizona in an uneasy microcosm of the American melting-pot ideal. Physical danger, distance from home, and military rigidity compounded the already strained new relationships. Because of the draft, most of these men had no choice but to serve in the armed forces. By the same token, they had no choice but to learn not only to live with men of different nationalities, classes, and religions, but to trust them with their lives. As any number of tough movie sergeants will tell you, the test of a fighting unit's effectiveness is the degree to which its members work together for the common good: completing the mission, and, if possible, surviving. If racial or religious prejudices arise when a troop comes under enemy fire, everyone's life is threatened and the mission may fail.

One social function of the World War II combat film, then, is the ritual integration of disparate communities into a cohesive whole—the fictional formation of an archetypal community within a small unit of soldiers. In film after film, Hollywood cast the war in stark but effective multicultural relief. *Bataan*, *Guadalcanal Diary*, and *The Purple Heart* each feature platoons with carefully tailored ethnic representations, a convention that survives in *Saving Private Ryan*. The platoon in 1944's *The Purple Heart*, for instance, features Captain Ross, Lieutenant Canelli, and Sergeants Clinton, Skvoznik, and Greenbaum. 1942's *Wake Island* even features a priggish *American* Corporal Goebbels for comic relief. The message was clear and emotionally gratifying to a nation at war, and it has remained so ever since: every race, class, and nationality in the country shared a commonality of purpose, a unity which distinguished Americans from the enemy. These demographically correct groups of buddies weren't designed solely for the GIs' benefit. They also taught the whole nation to respect each other's differences—to focus anger and fear not on other Americans but on the enemy, characteristically represented as an evil *Other*.

Because the combat film seems to pit "us" against "them," the concept of *Otherness* is especially useful in understanding the genre's dynamics. A theoretical concept of how human beings relate to one another, the theory of *Otherness* sees any "us against them" conflict to be rather a matter of "us vs. *not* us." In the case of World War II films, the Other—especially the Japanese —is defined not by what the Japanese are really like but rather by all the unspoken fears and desires one has about oneself. The Japanese thus become everything Americans are not: evil, deceitful, inhuman, monstrous. . . . Without minimizing or denying the real atrocities committed by Japanese forces during the war, it is worth noticing that the stock Japanese characters in American World War II combat films seem calculated to represent everything Americans saw as *un*American. Whether these traits are actually *Japanese* is another matter entirely.

The *ideological* function of these ethnically and racially mixed communities of soldiers becomes all the clearer in light of the fact that the American military was racially segregated at the time. The nation's need to stress democracy and equality thus overrode its actual military and cultural practice—an odd phenomenon indeed. African-American troops existed, but they were rarely if ever seen onscreen. The African-American soldiers who appear in *Bataan, Crash Dive,* and *Sahara* are not the norm. Most World War II combat films present as racially limited a vision of American culture as any other Hollywood genre, despite the combat film's explicit plea for unity, tolerance, and integration.

The "ideal" communities formed in the combat film are restrictive in other ways as well. There are never any gay soldiers in the combat film, though of course many thousands of gay GI's served their country in World War II. In this instance, the absence of an entire segment of the population from the screen has as much to do with Hollywood regulations as with military rules and cultural assumptions. Homosexuality was forbidden onscreen by the Production Code, not to mention the fact that the military commonly accepted—but officially denied—the existence of large numbers of gay soldiers. The rules of America's entertainment industry and military aside, however, the fact remains that the communities of soldiers depicted in the combat film, being almost entirely male, demonstrate a level of repressed homosexual tension that is unparalleled in any Hollywood genre. In other words, when buddies are under fire in the combat genre they often express their love for one another more or less directly, and both the depth of their emotions and their accompanying embarrassment are unusually noticeable.

Issues of race, prejudice, and suppressed messages intrude in the World War II combat film in still other ways. The two theaters of operation in the second World War had, in effect, two very different screens. In films about the war in Europe, Hollywood tended to present the conflict as one between two systems of government: democracy and fascism. But in films about the war in the Pacific, Hollywood often cast the conflict in terms of unmitigated racial terror—the vilification of the entire Japanese people, their customs and way of life. In World War II films, the Germans are generally seen as evil only insofar as they are Nazis; the Japanese, on the other hand, are evil because they are Japanese. Keep in mind that Hollywood did not instigate these prejudices. American culture of the period was full of blatant racial hate-mongering directed at the Japanese *as a race*. (After all, the United States had its own internment camps for its Japanese citizens.) What Hollywood did was to play upon these popular sentiments and thus give them wider, more prominent cultural force.

The World War II combat film implicitly questions the relationship of fiction and reality in the American cinema, since documentary footage of actual battles is often combined with fictional recreations and special effects. As a result, the history of the American combat film goes beyond issues of propaganda and patriotism to become a study in changing perceptions of realism.

The World War II combat film was strongly influenced by the techniques used by mobile camera crews that covered the war. After seeing *newsreels* of actual combat conditions, audiences were no longer satisfied by a Hollywood director's pure imagination on a studio back lot. Similarly, the intense television coverage of the Vietnam war made it impossible to represent Vietnam on movie screens without implicitly referring to the way the war looked on TV. In fact, the sudden shift toward location shooting during World War II might be seen as having prefigured the intense television coverage of Vietnam. If this is true, then the combat film has had far-reaching effects on world history. In any event, for any war film to succeed, it must be credible. But as always, credibility is in the eyes of the beholder; what one generation believes, succeeding generations may reject—all on the basis of what looks real and what does not. The combat film is a case in point.

This brief overview of war and American cinema has focused on only a few of the cultural and political aspects of the genre. The combat film offers some interesting aesthetic challenges as well. For one thing, the genre itself can be difficult to define. In a narrow view, the American combat film might be seen simply as a film about Americans in combat. In *American Cinema/American Culture*, John Belton takes a much broader and more complex view, seeing not only home-front melodramas such as *Since You Went Away* and *The Best Years of Our Lives* and the great *Casablanca* as war films but also various westerns. In this light, "spears and sandals" epics like *Spartacus*, *Alexander*, and *Troy* are combat films.

II. SCREENINGS

Here is a list of combat films made in a variety of periods about a variety of wars. Most are available on videotape or DVD:

Action in the North Atlantic (1943)
Air Force (1943)
Alexander (2004)
All Quiet on the Western Front (1930)
Apocalypse Now (1979)
Bataan (1943)
The Battle of Midway (documentary, 1942)
The Battle of Russia (documentary, 1943)
The Battle of San Pietro (documentary, 1945)
Black Hawk Down (2002)
The Big Parade (1925)
The Big Red One (1980)
Born on the Fourth of July (1989)
The Bridges at Toko-Ri (1955)
Casualties of War (1989)
Cry Havoc (1943)
The Deer Hunter (1978)
The Enemy Below (1957)
Fixed Bayonets (1951)
From Here to Eternity (1953)
Full Metal Jacket (1987)
Glory (1989)
The Great Escape (1963)
Guadalcanal Diary (1943)
Gung Ho! (1943)
Hamburger Hill (1987)
Home of the Brave (1949)
Immortal Sergeant (1943)
In Harm's Way (1965)
Let There Be Light (documentary, 1945)
The Longest Day (1962)
Memphis Belle (1990)
The Naked and the Dead (1958)
The Negro Soldier (documentary, 1944)
Patton (1970)
Platoon (1986)
Sands of Iwo Jima (1949)
Saving Private Ryan (1998)
Schindler's List (1993)
Sergeant York (1941)

A Soldier's Story (1984)
The Steel Helmet (1950)
They Were Expendable (1945)
The Thin Red Line (1998)
Thirty Seconds Over Tokyo (1944)
Three Kings (1999)
Tora! Tora! Tora! (1970)
Troy (2004)
Twelve O'Clock High (1949)
Verboten! (1959)
Wake Island (1942)
A Walk in the Sun (1946)
What Price Glory? (1926)
What Price Glory? (1952)

III. STUDY PLAN FOR THIS UNIT

Getting Started

1. Read Chapter 9: "War and Cinema," in *American Cinema/American Culture.*

2. If you have never seen any combat films, or have not seen one recently, take the time to screen at least one of the combat films listed above. Here are some suggestions for selecting a film:

   (a) It's likely that your familiarity with war-related films will be limited to relatively recent movies such as *Saving Private Ryan* or *Schindler's List*, both by Steven Spielberg. To get a better grasp of the genre's history, try an older film.

   (b) As always, keep an eye open for directors or stars whose work you have seen already. John Ford made a number of Westerns with which you may now be familiar, so Ford's *They Were Expendable* might be a good selection. You may have seen a Frank Capra comedy in Unit 6: "American Comedy"; Capra also directed the combat documentaries *Prelude to War*, *The Battle of Russia*, and *The Negro Soldier*. John Wayne, who figures prominently in the Western, appears in many combat films as well; see one of his war films for comparison and contrast (*They Were Expendable* works here as well, as does *Sands of Iwo Jima*).

Watching

1. As you watch the combat film, make a note of any impressions you have. As you now know from earlier units, it's not important if these ideas aren't worked out in detail; just get something down on paper to start with. For now, be particularly aware of ways in which the war film challenges your expectations:
   - If there are combat scenes, what do they look like? Are they rapidly cut or are they filmed in long takes? How are they lit?
   - Note who the main characters are, and how the film defines them. Is there one central hero, or does the film create a community of heroes?
   - Note how the film characterizes the enemy. How do the American characters describe this enemy? If the enemy appears, how does he look and act?
   - What is the film's attitude toward the war in question? Does the film serve a positive propaganda purpose, or is it critical of the war?

2. If you watch the telecourse program, take some notes about main ideas raised in the program, such as:
   - the "ideal platoon" made up of different races, religions, and ethnic groups;
   - the communal nature of heroism in some combat films;
   - the expressive nature of John Ford's and Samuel Fuller's combat films;
   - the influence of World War II newsreels on the combat film;
   - the mixed messages of certain combat films—the harshness of *Sands of Iwo Jima*'s story versus the film's heroic spectacle.
   - Note the title and a brief description of any film clips that attract your interest. These clips may later serve as the basis for a research paper.

For Further Study

1. Fill in the gaps in your notes. Note taking is a waste of time if you can't remember why you noted something, let alone if you can't read what you wrote.

2. Ask yourself:
   - How did the textbook, film, and telecourse program meet my expectations about war films? If this was my first experience with a war film, did the unit confirm any ideas I already had?
   - In what way were my expectations challenged? How did my learning experience change the way I think about war films? About war itself?

- Are there any questions that I might pursue in greater detail? Write them down in your notebook *now*.

IV. MEET THE EXPERTS

Lindsay Anderson, a British filmmaker and critic, directed *If . . .*, *Britannia Hospital*, and *Oh, Lucky Man*, among other films; he is also the author of the book *About John Ford*.

Thomas Doherty teaches English and American Studies at Brandeis University; he is the author of *Teenagers & Teenpics: The Juvenilization of American Movies in the 1950s* and *Projections of War: Hollywood and American Culture, 1941-1945*.

Chris Freitus, a lieutenant in the Marine Corps, teaches at the Marine Corps Basic School at Quantico.

Leonard Fribourg, a brigadier general in the Marine Corps, served as a technical advisor on *The Sands of Iwo Jima*.

Samuel Fuller directed some of the greatest low-budget films ever made, including the combat films *The Big Red One*, *The Steel Helmet*, and *Fixed Bayonets*.

Paul Fussell is the author of *The Great War in Modern Memory*, which won the National Book Award, as well as *Wartime: Understanding and Behavior in the Second World War*, *Class*, and *Bad: Or, the Dumbing of America*. He teaches English at the University of Pennsylvania.

Norm Hatch served as a combat photographer during World War II, shooting footage for the Academy Award-winning combat documentary *With the Marines at Tarawa*; he subsequently headed the Defense Department's Audio-Visual Division.

Joe Lombardi is a special effects expert whose credits include *Apocalypse Now*.

Anthony Lukeman is a lieutenant general in the United States Marine Corps.

Gene Michaud, a Vietnam-era veteran, served as the director of MIT's William Joiner Center for the Study of War and Its Social Consequences; he edited and contributed to the anthology *From Hanoi to Hollywood*.

Tim O'Brien, a Vietnam veteran, is the National Book Award-winning author of *Going After Cacciato* as well as *If I Die in a Combat Zone*, *The Things They Carried*, and *The Nuclear Age*.

Wayne Smith works with the Vietnam Veterans of America.

Oliver Stone served in the 25th Infantry Division in Vietnam, where he won the Bronze Star and the Purple Heart with Oak Leaf Cluster. He is the director of *Platoon*, *Born on the Forth of July*, *JFK*, *Salvador*, *The Doors*, and *Alexander*.

Bradley Vickers instructs marine recruits on moral leadership at the Officer Candidate School at Quantico.

William C. Westmoreland is a retired general of the United States Army; he served as a battalion commander in World War II, and as commander of United States forces in Vietnam.

Richard Zanuck is the Oscar-winning film producer responsible for *Driving Miss Daisy*, *Cocoon*, and *Rush*, among other films; his father, Daryl Zanuck, headed 20th Century-Fox from 1934 through 1956, and again in the mid-1960s.

V. SUGGESTED READINGS

Basinger, Jeanine. *The World War II Combat Film: Anatomy of a Genre*. New York: Columbia University Press, 1986. A critical survey of the genre, focusing on its recurrent themes and historical developments.

Boxwell, D. A. "Kulturkampf, Now and Then," *War, Literature, and the Arts* (Spring/Summer, 2000), pp. 122-35. An essay that traces contemporary American culture's use of war imagery and rhetoric.

Doherty, Thomas. *Projections of War: Hollywood and American Culture, 1941-1945*. New York: Columbia University Press, 1993. A cultural analysis of the genre, tying historical forces together with Hollywood representations.

Koppes, Clayton R., and Gregory D. Black. *Hollywood Goes to War: How Politics, Profits, and Propaganda Shaped World War II Movies*. Berkeley: University of California Press, 1990. A thematic and historical survey of the genre.

VI. EXERCISES AND ASSIGNMENTS

1. Consider the following basic scenario: In the midst of the war in Iraq, a group of three American soldiers advance toward an Iraqi position in Tikrit. The Americans engage a small group of Iraqis in combat, and after two hours of fighting the Iraqis surrender. Write two short treatments for this scenario—the first telling the story from the Americans' point of view, the second from the Iraqis'. The events should be identical; your descriptions of the characters, not to mention the emotional sense of the story, may change from treatment to treatment.

2. As an oral history project, conduct an interview with a family member or friend about his or her military experiences and the degree to which that person recognizes himself or herself in war films. Record the interview if possible; if you would like to turn it into an extensive research project, transcribe the interview and carefully edit it into a cohesive, readable form.

   Note: Conducting an interview of this sort is not as easy as it may seem at first. You must consider the issues on which you would like your subject to focus; you must research and prepare your questions in advance; and you must develop strategies of interaction. For instance, asking someone a simple, vague question like "What was it like during the war?" will likely result in an equally simple and vague response. A better approach is to research the war in question before the interview and begin the discussion with a concrete question, such as "Where were you stationed during the Gulf War, and why were you there?" Ask your subject about the friends he or she made during the war—where they came from, and what happened to them. Remember: you may be tempted simply to let the tape recorder roll and fade into the background, but you will almost certainly get more information from your subject if you take an active role in steering the conversation.

3. Both the textbook and the telecourse program present the Office of War Information as having attempted to ensure that Hollywood's accounts of World War II reflected America's best interests. Write a short essay—or a longer paper if you wish to pursue the question in detail—on the issue of government control of the film industry. Should the federal government ever control American entertainment? Is this in America's best interests? Who defines these interests? Does the fact of a war justify government control of the media? Support your argument with concrete details from history or current events. Develop hypothetical situations, and take a stand on the question. (For example, imagine the United States under attack from a foreign power; should Hollywood films continue to have the right to depict America in unflattering ways?)

4. Cultural history: To pursue the history of the American military's treatment of minority groups or the related history of ethnic, sexual, or racial representation in combat films, ask your librarian to help you find scholarly works on the subject. Read one or more of the works, and write a short book report on your findings. If you choose to pursue the topic in depth, write a 5–7 page research paper on the topic of your choice.

   Some important works on the subject include: "Movies, Race, and World War II," by Thomas Cripps, in the journal *Prologue* (Summer, 1982); "*The Negro Soldier* (1944): Film Propaganda in Black and White," also by Thomas Cripps, in *American Quarterly* 31, no. 5 (1979): 616–640;

and *Coming Out Under Fire*, a book-length history of gay men and lesbians in World War II, by Alan Bérubé. There are *many* other sources of information; ask your librarian for help in finding one on a topic that interests you.

Some notable films dealing with African-Americans and combat include *Home of the Brave* (1949), *A Soldier's Story* (1984), and the documentary *The Negro Soldier* (1944). For images of women at war, see *Cry Havoc* (1943) or *So Proudly We Hail* (1943). For images of repressed homosexuality, see *Wake Island* (1942) or *Guadalcanal Diary* (1943), among others. For images of the Japanese in the combat film, see almost any World War II film set in the Pacific.

VII. SELF TEST

1. Define or identify the following:
   (*a*) Office of War Information
   (*b*) "the ideal platoon"
   (*c*) newsreel
   (*d*) *Apocalypse Now*
   (*e*) Bataan
   (*f*) Samuel Fuller
   (*g*) Oliver Stone
   (*h*) pacifism

2. Which of the following makes this statement false? World War II combat films made during the war:
   (*a*) often vilified the German people as a race.
   (*b*) often expressed an apocalyptic sense of the irrationality of war in general.
   (*c*) always looked fake because they were invariably filmed in Hollywood soundstages.
   (*d*) were made for propaganda purposes.

3. Short answer: Note some of the ways in which the combat film *does not* conform to standard Hollywood filmmaking practice. Consider stylistic issues as well as questions of content.

4. True or false:
   (a) Although the armed forces were fully integrated during World War II, Hollywood's racism prevented African-Americans from participating onscreen.
   (b) Because women do not generally appear in the combat film, the genre is not concerned with sexuality.
   (c) An underlying logic of the World War II combat film is that of the reluctant warrior who hates war but learns to fight.
   (d) *Sergeant York* was an influential film because it showed the transformation of a war hero into a pacifist.

5. Essay: Why were newsreels important during World War II, and how did they influence the fictional combat film?

FILM NOIR

I. FILM NOIR: AN OVERVIEW

A cycle of unusually cynical, pessimistic, even paranoid Hollywood movies, most of which were made between the middle 1940s and the late 1950s, *film noir* is a stylistic blend of expressionism and realism, intense psychological examination, and shocking physical violence. Taken from the French, the term *film noir* translates literally as "black film." Putting aside the problematic racial ideology implicit in the link between blackness and evil, the term film noir is a signal that the world depicted onscreen is literally dark and shadowy. In noir films, such darkness is often downright fatal, its dense shadows suggesting the eternal night of death.

Double Indemnity, Crossfire, Out of the Past, In a Lonely Place, Touch of Evil— these are all classic noir films. Some are set in seedy bars and back alleys while others take place in a world of sleek, heartless glamour. But they all share a sense of moral compromise—of growing corruption, fatalism, and doom. Heroes are led astray, often by heroines; characters' motives are generally less than pure; and nobody comes out clean in the end. In short, noir films show us how easily the everyday world can turn nightmarish.

Film noir brings together several strains in cinema, literature, and world history. In Hollywood, the artistic movement known as *German Expressionism* had taken hold in the late 1920s and early 1930s, when European directors and technicians such as Fritz Lang (the director of the German Expressionist film *Metropolis* and the noir films *Scarlet Street* and *The Big Heat*, among others) and Karl Freund (who photographed *Metropolis*, the noir film *Key Largo*, and others) brought to the American film industry techniques in *cinematography, composition*, set design, and camera placement meant to render characters' internal psychological states in an external way. These methods included *low-key lighting*, sets built in distorted perspective, and exaggerated *high- and low-angle shots*.

In 1941, Orson Welles employed these techniques, together with unusually self-conscious *deep-focus* photography, in the filming of *Citizen Kane*, a key influence on film noir. *Citizen Kane* points the way to film noir not only in its moody visuals but also in its complex narrative structure, which employs flashbacks to evoke multiple points of view. Also in this period, the conventions of classical Hollywood cinema were beginning to be challenged by filmmakers who wanted to violate the codes of what might be called "high Hollywood"—the glossy studio sets, *high-key lighting*, glamorous costumes, and linear narrative structures that had come to define the American cinema in the 1930s. Crime films had been popular in the 1930s, but their heroes tended to be gentlemen, their villains flashy gangsters. Film noir was born out of the desire for grittier crime movies filmed with conventions thought to be more realistic—lower-key lighting, pettier criminals, more cynical detectives, and the grainier look of newsreel documentaries. As filmmaker Jean-Pierre Gorin admiringly puts it, film noir is a kind of "disreputable filmmaking."

Film noir's crime stories themselves grew out of literature. In the 1930s, authors such as Raymond Chandler, Dashiell Hammett, and James M. Cain wrote a series of highly successful "hard-boiled" crime novels—*The Maltese Falcon*, *The Postman Always Rings Twice*, *The Big Sleep*, and others—which were brought to the screen in the 1940s. The protagonists of these books are tough and streetwise, and they tend to use American vernacular language in a witty, stylized way. One example is this punchy turn of phrase near the end of Cain's *The Postman Always Rings Twice*, in which the doomed protagonist tries to understand how he got into trouble: "When I start to figure, it all goes blooey." In your textbook, John Belton quotes another example of self-consciously stylized, clever language from Billy Wilder's *Double Indemnity*. Wilder wants us to enjoy this interchange *as movie dialogue*—a better, more entertaining way of talking than we use in everyday life. Even in language, film noir is largely about *style*.

Because film noir is obsessed with murderous *femmes fatales*—evil, hateful women who seem to devote their lives to the destruction of men—some women may find these films offensive. As you will see, however, feminist critics often find film noir fascinating precisely for this reason. Like the rest of the film noir world, these killer blondes can be seen as representations of raging male paranoia. In this light, the contempt with which film noir tends to view women may really be a cover for a more profound and widespread psychosexual terror.

Beyond its cinematic and literary heritage, film noir developed out of World War II and the brutal nuclear legacy it spawned. It's not purely coincidental that the film noir cycle began at a time when millions of men and women were dying on the battlefield, in bombed out cities, and in concentration camp gas chambers. Many film noir heroes are themselves war veterans who return from the nightmare of global carnage to find that the seemingly innocent world back home has become dirty and corrupt. Given the threat of nuclear destruction that gripped the world after the bombing of Hiroshima and Nagasaki, it's not surprising that film noir is pervaded with a striking, almost cosmic paranoia. (This omnipresent anxiety is tied directly to the nuclear threat in the great 1955 film noir *Kiss Me Deadly*.)

Noir characters may often be returning soldiers for whom the trauma continues back home, but in the widest sense, it is really noir's mass audience and not simply a handful of film characters who tend to see the world as having become sullied and debased. Still, World War II only influenced the rise of film noir; it didn't produce film noir on its own. In fact, in addition to being a confluence of stylistic, literary, and historical trends, film noir is also a *phenomenological* effect—a product of the experience of watching films. Pursuing this line of thought, some critics have argued that film noir is not a genre at all but rather a mood—the anxious, fatalistic state of mind that certain films induce in audiences. These critics cite the fact that, generally speaking, Hollywood filmmakers didn't say to themselves, "Let's make a film noir" in the same deliberate way in which they set out to make Westerns, comedies, and combat films. According to these film historians, it is audience reactions—not social, historical, or artistic agendas—which define the cycle.

One way of defining film noir, then, is to see it as a collection of stylistic devices employed in a set of crime films made during and after World War II; in this case there can be no more noir films made today. A contrary approach is to see film noir as those films which produce a certain anxious *affect*, or emotional state, in audiences; in this sense, *Body Heat* and *Blue Velvet*, both made in the 1980s, and *L.A. Confidential* and *Red Rock West*, made in the 1990s, might be considered noir films even though they are both in color. John Belton calls these more recent films *"pseudo-noirs."* In addition, there have been several straight remakes of old noir films as well as looser reworkings of classics. In the former category, the 1947 film *Out of the Past* was remade in 1984 as *Against All Odds*. The 1946 film *The Postman Always Rings Twice* was remade in 1981; 1962's *Cape Fear*—a very late film in the original film noir cycle—was remade by Martin Scorsese in 1991; and the 1949 film *D.O.A.* was remade in 1988, also under its original title. In the category of reworked noir films, the best example is probably *Body Heat*, an update of the 1944 film *Double Indemnity*. And finally, there are a number of films which aren't remakes in any sense but which nevertheless draw heavily upon film noir's style and sense of moral ambiguity. *L.A. Confidential*, *Blue Velvet*, *Taxi Driver*, *Chinatown*, and even *Who Framed Roger Rabbit?* each employ images of urban corruption, restlessness, and despair in ways that consciously seek to remind audiences of the great noir films of the past.

In this way, the murkiness of the film noir world extends also to their study. Like the great noir detectives, students of film noir must first figure out what they're looking at because the evidence itself isn't crystal clear.

II. SCREENINGS

Here are two guides to film noir: one is a list of classics, the other a list of remakes, updates, and pseudo-noirs. Because they are newer, the films in the second list may be more accessible to you, not only in terms of seeing them on DVD or videotape but also in terms of enjoying them easily—of simply seeing what you are accustomed to seeing. But for the purposes of studying the

American cinema, it's worth the effort to view at least one example of film noir in its original historic and artistic form.

When watching original noir films, it's important to keep in mind that many were made with fairly small budgets. Some, like *Double Indemnity* and *The Big Sleep*, were big-budget productions with well known stars; others, like *Detour, Gun Crazy*, and *Pickup on South Street*, were made much more cheaply with lesser known actors. As a result, films like *Detour* simply won't have the extraordinary polish of newer, more expensive films like *L.A. Confidential* and *Chinatown*, and they ought not to be dismissed simply because they lack glossy production values. In fact, the drab graininess that comes from their low budgets is really part of their pleasure.

There is one other point to keep in mind: the way noir characters talk may strike you as funny, but don't worry. It's *supposed* to be fun. Film noir's tough-guy talk is colorful, clever, and, as you will hear, strangely idealized. Remember, these characters aren't meant to sound like ordinary people. Like a lot of Hollywood dialogue, film noir language is very style conscious. And what makes it so interesting, and so enjoyable, is that this high style is achieved by the use of low street slang—the speech of drunks, thieves, gangsters, and drug dealers. Notice, too, the rhythms of the heroes' speaking patterns. Just listen, for instance, to the poetic way Fred MacMurray says, in *Double Indemnity*, "We're both rotten, baby. Only you're a little *more* rotten."

Classic Noir Films:
The Asphalt Jungle (1950)
Beyond a Reasonable Doubt (1956)
The Big Heat (1953)
The Big Sleep (1946)
Clash by Night (1952)
Crossfire (1947)
Dark Passage (1947)
Detour (1945)
D.O.A. (1950)
Double Indemnity (1944)
Gilda (1946)
Gun Crazy (1949)
High Sierra (1941)
In a Lonely Place (1950)
Key Largo (1948)
The Killers (1946)
The Killing (1956)
Kiss Me Deadly (1955)
Lady in the Lake (1947)
The Lady from Shanghai (1948)
Laura (1944)
The Maltese Falcon (1941)

Murder, My Sweet (1944)
The Naked City (1948)
The Naked Kiss (1965)
Out of the Past (1947)
The Postman Always Rings Twice (1946)
Scarlet Street (1945)
Shadow of a Doubt (1943)
Sorry, Wrong Number (1948)
The Stranger (1946)
Strangers on a Train (1951)
Sweet Smell of Success (1958)
They Live by Night (1948)
Touch of Evil (1958)
Underworld, USA (1961)
White Heat (1949)
The Woman in the Window (1944)
The Wrong Man (1956)

Some Film Noir Remakes, Updates, and Pseudo-Noirs:
Against All Odds (1984)
Blood Simple (1984)
Blue Velvet (1986)
Body Heat (1981)
Cape Fear (1992)
Chinatown (1974)
Dirty Harry (1971)
D.O.A. (1988)
Farewell, My Lovely (1975)
L.A. Confidential (1997)
The Long Goodbye (1973)
The Man Who Wasn't There (2001)
Night Moves (1975)
The Postman Always Rings Twice (1981)
Taxi Driver (1976)
Tightrope (1984)
Who Framed Roger Rabbit? (1988)

III. STUDY PLAN FOR THIS UNIT

Getting Started

1. Read Chapter 10: "Film Noir: Somewhere in the Night," and Chapter 12: "Hollywood and the Cold War," in *American Cinema/American Culture*.

2. Watch at least one of the classic noir films, listed above. Many of them are available on DVD and videotape (but beware of colorized versions, especially since a key element of film noir's style is its black-and-white cinematography).

Watching

1. As you watch the noir film you have selected, write down any ideas or impressions you have and make a note of scenes that strike your interest. Notice in particular how the film *looks* and *sounds*:
   - Jot down a few words to describe the setting and lighting style of any scenes that catch your eye.
   - Write a very short description of the main characters—who they are and what they look like.
   - If a character utters a particularly colorful line of dialogue, write it down.
   - Listen to the music on the sound track; write a few words to describe it.

2. Take general notes about one or more of the central ideas raised in the telecourse program, such as:
   - the effects of World War II on American cinema;
   - the influence of hard-boiled detective fiction;
   - the expressive look of film noir lighting, and the ways in which cinematographers achieve it;
   - the psychological elements of film noir.

3. If one of these topics strikes you as particularly interesting, it might serve as the subject for a paper. More detailed note taking on this subject would be worthwhile.

4. Note the title and a short description of any film clips that particularly attract your interest. For example: "*Lady from Shanghai*—Welles—murder, mirrors, crashing." Later, you can try to see this film on DVD or videotape and do some further reading about it.

For Further Study

1. Before too much time elapses after reading the textbook and viewing the program, fill in any gaps in your notes.

2. Ask yourself the following questions:
   - In what way were my expectations about film noir fulfilled? Do 1940s and 1950s crime dramas look and sound the way I thought they would?
   - In what way were my expectations challenged? Did I think these films would be more violent or less violent? Was I surprised at their moral ambiguity, or did I expect them to depict the world as essentially corrupt and threatening?
   - Is there an aspect to film noir that I would like to pursue further? If something has already struck you as interesting, write it down now. With the program fresh in your mind, remember the points it raises and note as many as possible on paper so that later, when you begin to write about film noir, you'll have a ready-made guide from which to begin.

IV. MEET THE EXPERTS

Paul Arthur teaches courses in film at Montclair State College and is the author of *Shadows on the Mirror: Film Noir and the Cold War in America 1945-1951*.

John Bailey is an award-winning cinematographer whose work includes *Ordinary People, American Gigolo, The Big Chill,* and *The Accidental Tourist*.

Albert Bezzerides wrote *Kiss Me Deadly*, the classic noir film directed by Robert Aldrich.

Kathryn Bigelow has directed feature films in several genres, including the vampire film *Near Dark*, the police thriller *Blue Steel*, and the road movie *The Loveless*.

Andre de Toth directed the noir films *Pitfall* and *Crime Wave*; he is best known for directing the spectacular 3-D film *House of Wax*.

Edward Dmytryk directed over 50 feature films, including the classic noir films *Murder, My Sweet* and *Crossfire*. One of the so-called Hollywood Ten, Dmytryk was imprisoned for refusing to testify before the House Un-American Activities Committee.

Otto Friedrich, a historian, is the author of *City of Nets: A Portrait of Hollywood in the 1940s*.

Martin Goldsmith produced the films *Detour*, *Shakedown*, The *Narrow Margin*, and *Hell's Island*.

Jean-Pierre Gorin is a filmmaker and critic, the director of *Poto and Cabengo* and, with Jean-Luc Godard, *Tout va bien* and *Letter to Jane*.

Ron Goulart is the author of *Cheap Thrills: An Informal History of Pulp Magazines* and *The Dime Detectives*, as well as over 250 mystery stories.

Lawrence Kasdan directed such films as *Body Heat*, *The Big Chill*, *The Accidental Tourist*, *Grand Canyon*, and *Dreamcatcher*.

Joseph Lewis is best known for directing *Gun Crazy*, though he also directed many other fascinating low-budget films.

Errol Morris directed the award-winning documentary *The Thin Blue Line* as well as *Gates of Heaven* and *Fog of War*.

Janey Place wrote the essays "Some Visual Motifs in Film Noir" and "Women in Film Noir" as well as two books on John Ford.

Abraham Polonsky wrote and directed the noir film *Force of Evil*. He was blacklisted by the film industry after refusing to testify before the House Un-American Activities Committee.

Paul Schrader, a critic, screenwriter, and director, wrote the essay "Notes on Film Noir" as well as a book on the directors Yasujiro Ozu, Robert Bresson, and Carl-Theodor Dreyer; he directed *Hard Core*, *American Gigolo*, *Cat People*, *Mishima*, *Patty Hearst*, *The Comfort of Strangers*, and *Auto Focus*.

Martin Scorsese directed the noir-influenced films *Taxi Driver*, *After Hours*, and *Cape Fear* as well as *Goodfellas*, *Raging Bull*, *The King of Comedy*, *New York, New York*, *The Last Temptation of Christ*, *The Age of Innocence*, *Kundun*, *Gangs of New York*, and *The Aviator*.

Marie Windsor starred in many Hollywood films, including *Force of Evil*, *The Narrow Margin*, *The Sniper*, *The Killing*, *Bedtime Story*, and *Abbott and Costello Meet the Mummy*.

V. SUGGESTED READINGS

Dickos, Andrew. *Street with No Name: A History of the Classic American Film Noir*. Lexington: University of Kentucky Press, 2002. A fine survey of the genre.

Hirsch, Foster. *Film Noir: The Dark Side of the Screen*. New York: Da Capo Press, 1983. An illustrated survey of the genre, with short analyses of individual films and an extensive filmography.

Kaplan, E. Ann, ed. *Women in Film Noir*. New York: New York Zoetrope, 1980. A collection of feminist criticism of film noir, both of individual films and the genre as a whole.

Krutnick, Frank. *In a Lonely Street: Film Noir, Genre, Masculinity*. London: Routledge, 1991. An intriguing theoretical approach to the genre and its gender issues.

Schrader, Paul. "Notes on Film Noir," in Barry Keith Grant, ed., *Film Genre Reader*. Austin: University of Texas Press, 1986. A seminal essay on the genre, outlining its essential thematic and stylistic elements.

VI. EXERCISES AND ASSIGNMENTS

1. Create your own film noir sequence out of the following basic situation: An older man and a younger woman are having a conversation in which the woman becomes increasingly angry; at the end of the sequence, her anger becomes explosive.
   - First: Decide who these characters are. What is their relationship to each other? Father and daughter? Uncle and niece? Businessman and prostitute? Teacher and student? Give them any identities you wish.
   - Next: Create a setting for these characters. Where are they? What is the *mise-en-scene*? Does the scene occur inside or outside? Is it a public place, like a restaurant or bar? If so, is it crowded or empty? Clean or dirty? Attractive or ugly? Or is it inside a private space—a bedroom? If so, *whose* bedroom? How is it decorated? (Since you do not have to worry about the budget of this film, be as creative a set decorator as you like.)
   - How is the room lit? Remember, lighting is an important feature of film noir.
   - What are they wearing?
   - What are they arguing about? First decide on a general subject—money, love, sex, crime, a child, a grade—and then, once you have narrowed it down, begin to write some lines of dialogue about this topic.
   - How does the scene end? What does the woman finally do to express her anger? Remember, this is a film noir sequence, so you can be as violent as you like.
   - Finally: Design a simple sequence of shots for this bit of narrative. Place the camera anywhere you'd like, move it whenever you want, and cut to another shot whenever you think it's appropriate. Or, if you decide to film the whole bit in a single take, note where the camera is placed at all times.

2. *(a)* Watch the opening sequence of a classic film noir and describe it in detail. Pick out as many filmic elements as you can: what the image contains, where the camera is, whether the camera moves and when, what the lighting looks like, what characters say, and so on. Be precise, descriptive, and detailed; do not take any element of mise-en-scene for granted.

(b) From the details you gather in your description, write a two- to three-page paper about what the opening sequence means in terms of the overall film. Why does the film begin as it does? How do the first few shots of the film relate to the last few? What are the major themes in the film? Does the opening sequence set up these themes? If so, how?

3. In the telecourse program, Paul Schrader describes the "black widow" nature of many of film noir's female characters as resulting from social changes in the postwar era, when soldiers returned from the battlefields to find that women had become more independent in their absence. Schrader suggests that on a wide cultural level men not only feared women's new-found economic status, since many women had taken jobs during World War II, but also the threat of unfaithfulness on the part of wives and girlfriends. According to Schrader, this tension led to the double threat of money and sex expressed in film noir.

Write a paper on the ways in which women's roles may have shifted during World War II. Base your observations on solid research, using the following suggestions as a way of getting started.
- Find out what historians have to say on this issue by looking up books and articles on the subject. (Ask the librarian for research assistance if you need it.) Keep in mind that all historians may not agree on this issue. You may want to find two who disagree and structure your paper as an argument between these differing points of view.
- See how popular magazines of the period depict women in magazine articles and advertising. (Most libraries have collections of such contemporary magazines as *Look*, *Life*, *Time*, and the *Saturday Evening Post*.) Keep in mind that because the issue of gender roles is complicated, one or two pictures of women will not be enough to tell you about how women were really viewed at the time. A better approach would be to find a *variety* of images, and compare and contrast them.

4. In the telecourse program, the development of film noir is tied into the rise of the so-called McCarthy hearings, in which Congress investigated the influence of communism on the Hollywood film industry. Here are several ways of pursuing this topic in more detail:
   - Write a short paper (2 or 3 pages) outlining the rise of McCarthyism. Who were the Hollywood Ten? How was the filmmaking industry affected by this inquiry?
   - The program links McCarthyism specifically with Orson Welles's film noir *Touch of Evil*. See *Touch of Evil* and write a short paper about how the film deals with McCarthyism. (Note: you may come to believe that the film is actually not about McCarthyism; do not be afraid to pursue this line of argument.)

VII. SELF TEST

1. Define or identify the following:
   (a) cinematography
   (b) German Expressionism
   (c) deep focus
   (d) Joseph McCarthy
   (e) Orson Welles
   (f) *Detour*
   (g) James M. Cain
   (h) realism

2. Which of the following makes this statement false? Film noir was strongly influenced by:
   (a) the changing role of women in the post-war era.
   (b) the atomic bombing of Hiroshima and Nagasaki.
   (c) lighting techniques originally developed in Japan.
   (d) communists working as screenwriters in Hollywood.

3. Short answer: In the program, the writer Martin Goldsmith says of the novelist James M. Cain, "He wrote with a meat cleaver." What does Goldsmith mean, not only in terms of Cain himself but of film noir writing in general?

4. True or false:
   (a) The term *film noir* originally referred to French films made after World War II.
   (b) *Citizen Kane*'s linear narrative structure was a profound influence on film noir.
   (c) The directors Edgar Ulmer, Billy Wilder, and Fritz Lang began their careers in Germany and moved to Hollywood after World War II.
   (d) German Expressionism seeks to express internal psychological states in an external way, through set design, lighting, and camera angle.

5. Essay: In the telecourse program, the cinematographer John Bailey says, "There is an element in film noir, in the way light and shadow is used in such extreme contrast, that is almost religious or spiritual or philosophical." What does Bailey mean by this? How can a Hollywood movie be considered to be philosophical? Do you agree with Bailey's vision of film noir as an encounter between good and evil, and that this moral undercurrent accounts for the use of strong black and white cinematography?

HOLLYWOOD IN THE AGE OF TELEVISION

I. HOLLYWOOD IN THE AGE OF TELEVISION: AN OVERVIEW

If the American film industry of the 1950s could be summed up in a single word, that word might be "breakdown." Industrially, commercially, emotionally, sexually, and culturally, the whole Hollywood system fragmented in the '50s. In many ways it never fully recovered.

Discussions of Hollywood in the 1950s typically cite the abrupt and rapid rise of television to explain the breakdown of the American film industry. In fact, television simply helped fuel American audiences' shift from regular moviegoing to less frequent attendance. The rabbit-ear antennas that pulled in television signals in the 1950s did indeed multiply like rabbits across the new suburban landscape, and by the end of the decade they enabled most Americans to watch moving images without leaving their homes. For studio executives, these proliferating TV sets may have symbolized their industry's problems, but the symbol was a false excuse for more complicated troubles.

Until the late 1940s, Hollywood was a relatively streamlined, efficient industry dominated by a handful of corporations that not only cranked out a steady stream of films but also exhibited those films in their own chains of theaters. Suddenly, in a matter of years, the whole system crumbled. In 1948, an important Supreme Court decision, *United States v. Paramount Pictures, Inc., et al.*, forced the studios to divest themselves of their theaters on the grounds that the old system was an oligopoly. Independent producers, now on more equal footing, could compete with the studios more vigorously than ever.

At the same time, America's suburbs were growing, taking people further away from the big old movie palaces downtown. And postwar consumers began spending their leisure time and money differently than they had during the movies' golden age as the experience of "going out" changed in the postwar era. Television was taking the place of movies for the purposes of passive entertainment, and when consumers went out they increasingly preferred more active forms of leisure activity. Hollywood could no longer count on a regular mass audience.

Movie attendance did not decline across the board, however. Teenagers had access to more money than ever before, and in terms of sheer numbers there were simply more teenagers than ever. Teens suddenly became a massive consumer market of their own, and a whole new type of film began to be made specifically for them—*The Blackboard Jungle*, *Rock Around the Clock*, and a host of *schlock* movies with titles like *Teenage Crime Wave* and *Teenage Caveman*. They were relatively inexpensive to produce (when they weren't downright cheap), so they didn't usually lose money. For producers, this was the key.

Meanwhile, Hollywood sexual mores began to shift. The Production Code, which had enforced a rigid set of onscreen dos and don'ts since 1934, began to collapse as directors and audiences grew weary of the Code's antiseptic vision of life (no crimes that pay, no adultery, no nudity, no homosexuality, no ridiculing of religion and the rule of law, and so on). As if on cue, the independent producers who benefited from the collapse of the studio system began to provide audiences with increasingly explicit sexuality in films, not to mention an array of new technologies designed to lure audiences back into movie theaters. Sexually charged problem dramas such as *Rebel Without a Cause* starring James Dean and lurid sex farces such as *The Girl Can't Help It* with Jane Mansfield and an all-star lineup of rock-and-roll greats provided audiences with something they could not find on television, and often they did so through the formally innovative means of new widescreen processes—CinemaScope, VistaVision, Panavision, and others.

The technological innovations of the 1950s set the stage for later developments in sound quality, as Hollywood continued to find ways of distinguishing moviegoing from watching television. Of these, the *Dolby system* is the most well-known and influential. The process, invented by Ray Dolby and introduced in films in 1976, reduces background noise and thereby produces clearer recording and playback with greater fidelity to the original sound. Other developments include *stereophonic sound*, *surround sound*, and *digital recording*, all of which give audiences an experience of clear, loud, acoustically rich sound that cannot be reproduced at home on television. In fact, it's worth noting that the use of stereo sound on film sound tracks actually preceded its use in the record industry.

In the 1950s, a number of important film directors such as John Ford, Alfred Hitchcock, Howard Hawks, Billy Wilder, Nicholas Ray, Douglas Sirk, Frank Tashlin, Samuel Fuller, and Vincente Minnelli hit their artistic stride at precisely the time when the range of cinematic technology and subject matter was expanding dramatically. Hollywood may have broken down, but the breakdown proved to be healthy for both its art and its commerce. Hitchcock's *Psycho* (1960), Ford's *The Searchers* (1956), Hawks's *Rio Bravo* (1959), Wilder's *Some Like It Hot* (1959), Ray's *Bigger Than Life* (1956), and Sirk's *Written on the Wind* (1958) are only a few of the outstanding films produced during the period of Hollywood's so-called decline.

In the telecourse program for this unit, you will learn about some of the other directors of this period—Arthur Penn, John Frankenheimer, Delbert Mann, and Sidney Lumet. These directors began their careers in New York at a time when almost all network television was produced there, and they brought to the new medium a New York sensibility and style influenced by the prevailing tastes in theater and literature in the period—specifically, a penchant for gritty realism.

Mann's live television production of writer Paddy Chayevsky's *Marty* was something of a landmark in small-scale dramas about characters perceived to be ordinary citizens. This ordinariness was conveyed artistically not only by its black-and-white photography but also by costume and speech pattern: Marty, played by Ernest Borgnine, wore an undershirt and talked the way working-class men are sometimes thought to talk. *Marty* was later turned into a feature film in an odd sort of truce between the two competing media. Not only did *Marty* suggest that television and film were more compatible than anyone had thought, but it also impressed critics who saw it as evidence of Hollywood's ability to reject spectacle and technology in favor of character and story.

In fact, "story," "character," and "people" became a kind of mantra among the New York television crowd. Director Sidney Lumet went so far as to say that CinemaScope was a futile and misguided invention because films were about people and people were not wider than they were tall. But, as critic Charles Barr has pointed out, books do not have to be in the shape of their subjects either. Moreover, Hollywood films had always attempted to integrate spectacle with story, technology with character.

In retrospect, the character-oriented realism of the television directors was an artistic convention particular to its time and place. Today, *Marty* appears as stylized in its own way as *The Ten Commandments* or *Ben-Hur*. And even those television directors who went on to direct Hollywood features embraced spectacle and technology as well as story and character. Frankenheimer's *The Manchurian Candidate*, Penn's *Bonnie and Clyde*, and even Lumet's *The Wiz* all stand as evidence of Hollywood's ability to blend technology and story. In the final analysis, the artistic influence of television on film has proven to be minor.

II. SCREENINGS

A huge number of films could serve as appropriate screenings for this unit, from the mammoth biblical epics and wild teen exploitation films of the 1950s to the science-fiction extravaganzas and horror films of the more recent past. However, since every film produced in the United States after 1953 has been in one widescreen form or another, and since many video distributors have simply altered the format of these films when releasing them on videotape (thereby chopping off anywhere from a quarter to half the image so that it fits the shape of the television set), we cannot recommend that you view many of these films on video unless you are sure that they are letterboxed. You will be missing precisely those elements of the films that were created to make them *different* from television.

Since much of the textbook chapter concerns widescreen processes, this screenings list focuses on widescreen films. Several others (*Psycho* and *Rock Around the Clock*, for instance) are included because they offered audiences of the 1950s and early 1960s levels of violence and teenage rebellion that could not be found on television. And finally, a selection of films by some of the directors noted in the program are listed. Many DVD versions of widescreen films may be found in the correct aspect ratio.

The Apartment (1960)
Apocalypse Now (1979)
Bells Are Ringing (1960)
Ben-Hur (1959)
Bonnie and Clyde (1967)
A Bucket of Blood (1959)
Bye Bye Birdie (1963)
Chinatown (1974)
Forbidden Planet (1956)
High School Confidential (1958)
Home from the Hill (1959)
Invasion of the Body Snatchers (1956)
It's Always Fair Weather (1955)
Lawrence of Arabia (1962)
The Longest Day (1962)
Love Me or Leave Me (1955)
Lust for Life (1956)
The Manchurian Candidate (1962)
Manhattan (1979)
Marty (1955)
The Naked Kiss (1965)
New York, New York (1977)
North By Northwest (1959)
Psycho (1960)
Raiders of the Lost Ark (1981)
Rock Around the Clock (1956)
Some Came Running (1958)
Some Like It Hot (1959)
Spartacus (1960)
Tea and Sympathy (1956)
2001: A Space Odyssey (1968)
What Ever Happened to Baby Jane? (1962)
The Wild One (1953)

III. STUDY PLAN FOR THIS UNIT

Getting Started

1. Read Chapter 13: "Hollywood in the Age of Television," in *American Cinema/American Culture.*

2. Select one of the films in the "Screenings" list above. Or, if you live in an area with a theater that shows classic films, take the time to see an older film on a large screen. Even if the film isn't from the 1950s or later, you will still get the experience of seeing a classic film in the way it was meant to be seen. Or, finally, just go to the movies! See a big, new expensive Hollywood film—preferably in a theater equipped with great sound equipment, so you can hear what you are missing every time you wait for a film to come out on video or show up on television.

Watching

1. As you watch the film you have selected, jot down any ideas or impressions you have. Be especially aware of how the film *looks* and *sounds*:
   - Note the colors and lighting effects films can achieve, and be aware of how much more intense they are than anything you see on a television screen.
   - See if there are any ideas or situations in the film that would not appear on network television. (These may include—but are not limited to—images of graphic violence and explicit sex.)
   - Be aware of the shape of the screen. If you are watching a widescreen film, see if (and how) the director encourages you to notice the horizontality of the image.
   - Listen to the music and sound effects, especially if you are seeing the film in a movie theater. Compare these effects to TV.

2. Take some notes about one or more of the central ideas discussed in the telecourse program, such as:
   - the impact of New York theater on Hollywood;
   - the changing conceptions of realism in the 1950s, and the stylistic devices directors employed to provide a sense of realism;
   - the so-called golden age of live television in the 1950s;
   - the extraordinary popularity of spectacle films during the 1950s, and the challenge offered by smaller-scale dramas;
   - the identities and directing philosophies of directors who moved from television to feature filmmaking in the 1950s.

3. As always, think about topics to develop into a research paper or class presentation. This unit's topic should provide you with some new and perhaps more colorful ideas.

For Further Study

1. Fill in the gaps in your notes.

2. Reconsider the program in light of your own experience:
   - Did the program change the way you look at movies?
   - Did the program change the way you think about television?

3. Write a review of the film you saw, putting your new knowledge of cinema to practice. Go beyond saying whether you liked the movie or not; evaluate the direction, the cinematography, and the score.

IV. MEET THE EXPERTS

Robert Altman worked on such television series as *Combat*, *Bonanza*, and *Alfred Hitchcock Presents* before moving on to direct such films as *M*A*S*H*, *McCabe and Mrs. Miller*, *Nashville*, *The Player*, and *Gosford Park*.

Mark Canton is a second-generation Hollywood executive; he was at one time the head of Columbia Pictures.

Raymond Carney teaches film courses at Boston University; he is the author of books on Frank Capra and John Cassavetes.

Charles Champlin is a film critic for the *Los Angeles Times*.

Peter Falk is the star of the *Columbo* segments of "NBC Sunday Mystery Movie" as well as such films as *A Woman Under the Influence*, *It's a Mad, Mad, Mad, Mad World*, and *Wings of Desire*.

John Frankenheimer, who began his directing career with television dramas in the 1950s, went on to direct such feature films as *The Manchurian Candidate* and *Seven Days in May*.

Todd Gitlin teaches courses in television at the University of California at Berkeley; he is the author of *Inside Prime Time* and *The Sixties: Years of Hope, Days of Rage*, among other books.

Sidney Lumet is the director of such films as *12 Angry Men*, *Serpico*, *Dog Day Afternoon*, and *Network*.

Delbert Mann directed both the television and feature film versions of *Marty*, as well as such films as *Lover Come Back* and *That Touch of Mink*.

Arthur Penn directed many live television dramas and went on to direct such feature films as *Bonnie and Clyde*, *The Miracle Worker*, and *Little Big Man*.

Jonas Rosenfield, a past director of marketing for both 20th Century-Fox and Columbia Pictures, is president of International Film Marketing Company.

Gena Rowlands starred in several films by her husband, John Cassavetes, including *A Woman Under the Influence* and *Gloria*, as well as such films as *Once Around* and *Tony Rome*.

Gene Siskel appeared as a movie reviewer on the television show *Siskel and Ebert*.

Aaron Spelling is the producer of many successful television series, including *Charlie's Angels*, *The Love Boat*, *The Mod Squad*, and *Beverly Hills 90210*.

Haskell Wexler wrote, directed, and served as cinematographer of the film *Medium Cool*; he also photographed such films as *One Flew Over the Cuckoo's Nest*, *Matewan*, and *Bound for Glory*.

V. SUGGESTED READINGS

Barnouw, Erik. *Tube of Plenty: The Evolution of American Television*. New York: Oxford University Press, 1982. A history of TV, from its invention through the early 1980s.

Barr, Charles. "CinemaScope: Before and After," *Film Quarterly 16*, no. 4. Reprinted in Gerald Mast and Marshall Cohen, eds., *Film Theory and Criticism*. The seminal essay on the aesthetics of widescreen cinema.

Belton, John. *Widescreen Cinema*. Cambridge: Harvard University Press, 1992. An excellent and detailed look at the history and aesthetics of CinemaScope, VistaVision, Panavision, Cinerama, and other widescreen processes.

Doherty, Thomas. *Teenagers and Teenpics: The Juvenilization of American Movies in the 1950s*. Winchester, MA: Unwin Hyman, 1988. A critical yet appreciative scholarly survey of films pitched to teenagers in the 1950s.

Macdonald, Dwight. "A Caste, A Culture, A Market—I," *The New Yorker* (November 22, 1958): 57-94. The first of a two-part essay on the burgeoning teen market of the 1950s—a critically astute commentary on one aspect of American culture in the period.

Warshow, Robert. *The Immediate Experience: Movies, Comics, Theatre, and Other Aspects of Popular Culture*. New York: Doubleday, 1962. A series of essays written by an articulate critic of popular culture in the late 1940s and 1950s.

VI. EXERCISES AND ASSIGNMENTS

1. As a way of understanding motion pictures and their relationship to video and television, make a list of the films you have seen in theaters in the past six months. Ask yourself why you chose each film. Was it the film's stars? Its director? Good reviews? Advertising? Recommendations of friends? Write your responses down. Then list the films you have seen on video, and ask yourself the same questions. Finally, list the films you have seen on television (either on cable or network), and ask yourself the same set of questions.

   Compare these lists and your responses. What conclusions are you able to draw from them? For example, were there any films on the videotape or television lists that you had decided not to see in the theater because you knew it would be available soon on videotape? Did the videos you rented or bought tend to be older films which were not available for viewing in theaters? Ask yourself whether your own film-viewing patterns are typical or atypical. Draw some tentative conclusions about film in the video age from your own experience. (Note: This exercise depends upon your ability to stand back from yourself a bit and analyze your own movie-viewing habits. To make the exercise work effectively, you must treat it more seriously than you would a simple opinion survey.)

2. (a) To see the aesthetics of CinemaScope or Panavision in an active way, draw five identical stick figures on a plain sheet of paper, and draw five identical faces on another sheet. Frame each of these figures and faces differently: use circles, ovals, squares, and rectangles, each in a different size. Look at how each frame subtly changes the way you perceive your drawings. Imagine that these drawings are film images, and imagine the background between the frame and the figure.

   (b) Next, draw two identical faces on a plain sheet of paper. Around one of the faces, draw a rectangle in (roughly) the Academy aspect ratio of 1.33:1 (for every inch of height there will be 1.3 inches of width); around another face draw a rectangle representing the CinemaScope aspect ratio of 2.35:1 (for every inch of height there will be 2.35 inches of width). Fill in identical backgrounds to each drawing.

   (c) Relate these drawings to the textbook's discussion of CinemaScope and other widescreen processes. How much more background do you see in the 'Scope drawing? How does this affect the figure in the frame? Think in terms of spatial relationships.

   (d) Now design a film sequence around your 'Scope drawing. Who would the character be? What would the background be? Would there be anyone else in the image? In what direction would the character be looking, and what would he or she see? Draw the character's line of vision with a series of dotted lines. What might the next shot contain? Draw it, and see how the two shots might be edited together.

3. As an exercise in cultural history and practical criticism, find Dwight Macdonald's "A Caste, A Culture, A Market," listed above in "Suggested Readings." In the essay, Macdonald examines America's new youth culture from a variety of perspectives. Write a 5-page paper comparing Macdonald's view of the youth culture of the 1950s with the youth culture of today. Has the situation changed? *Be sure to back up your argument with concrete examples*, not only from Macdonald's essay but from the world around you.

4. Closely analyze a widescreen film sequence. Pay particular attention to the composition of the images and the spatial relationships created by the extended horizontal framing. As you can see in the "Screenings" list provided in section II, above, as well as in the lists provided throughout the study guide, many widescreen films are available on DVD in the correct aspect ratio as well as letterboxed DVDs. Some cable television stations show widescreen films in the correct aspect ratio.

VII. SELF TEST

1. Define or identify the following:
   (a) anamorphic lens
   (b) *United States v. Paramount Pictures, Inc., et al.*
   (c) letterbox
   (d) Production Code
   (e) Cinerama
   (f) 3-D
   (g) aspect ratio
   (h) James Dean

2. Which of the following makes this statement false? In the 1950s, television in the United States:
   (a) was mostly limited to situation comedies like *I Love Lucy* and *Father Knows Best*, leaving gritty dramas to the movies.
   (b) is almost entirely to blame for the declining box-office returns of Hollywood films.
   (c) provided a training ground for writers and directors who went on to direct Hollywood feature films.
   (d) was considered to be a passing cultural fad; nobody took it seriously as a means of communication.

3. Short answer: What happens when widescreen films are shown on television in the incorrect aspect ratio?

4. True or false:
   (a) Weekly motion picture attendance hit its peak of 95 million in 1929; in 1953, the figure was less than half of that.
   (b) Unlike 3-D, Cinerama was a fairly inexpensive process in terms of production and exhibition; the problem was that audiences disliked the way Cinerama films looked.
   (c) Todd-AO was a gimmicky process that failed artistically and commercially because audiences preferred the film image to be a more normal size.
   (d) Drive-in theaters were popular in the 1950s not only because they were cheap to build but also because they solved the problem of finding a baby sitter.

5. Essay: Why might a director choose to film in widescreen? Describe some of the virtues and limitations of widescreen films, and make an argument for or against the use of widescreen.

6. Extra credit: What do the initials DVD stand for?

THE FILM SCHOOL GENERATION

I. THE FILM SCHOOL GENERATION: AN OVERVIEW

What makes a great film director? This is an impossible question to answer in prescriptive terms. After all, if there was a handy road map to point the way to artistic and commercial success, the cinema would have many more great directors. Even on a descriptive level, too, it is difficult to explain exactly why some directors are able to maintain long, productive, and creative careers while others choke on their first directing assignment and never get another chance. Because of the necessary mix of talent and luck, the making of a great director is not something that can be easily spelled out in a recipe.

The question is more readily answered in historical terms. This unit explores how and why a certain group of young directors rose to prominence in the late 1960s and early 1970s. What changed in Hollywood and in American culture to enable these particular directors (known collectively as the "New Hollywood") to make commercially successful and critically respected films at this time? What are the stylistic and thematic echoes in these films—not only to each other but to the whole history of Hollywood? And what do these directors have to say about the art of the cinema? Do they see themselves as challenging or embracing classical Hollywood style? And who are the film school directors of today?

From the early years of the American cinema through the studio era, directors became directors by various routes. Sometimes, as in the cases of D. W. Griffith, Charles Chaplin, Buster Keaton, and others, their careers as stage actors led them to perform in films and later to direct them. (Keaton was usually not credited as the director of his films, but at the peak of his career he nevertheless maintained creative control.) Others, like George Cukor, Orson Welles, and Elia Kazan, were successful New York theater directors before moving on to films. Some, like Arthur Penn and Blake Edwards, started out in television production. Still others took more circuitous routes. John Ford arrived in Hollywood because his brother, an actor, promised to help him find work; Ford began his film career as a stunt man, learning to direct films literally from the bottom up. Action film director Allan Dwan was a lighting engineer who helped develop the mercury vapor arc lamp used in early silent films. After installing some arc lamps for the Essanay studio, Dwan sold the company 15 scripts. Later, at another studio, Dwan became a director one day when the person originally assigned the task showed up drunk.

Now consider this: Martin Scorsese, Steven Spielberg, George Lucas, Francis Coppola, Paul Schrader, John Milius, Brian De Palma, Kathryn Bigelow, Robert Zemeckis, Spike Lee, David Lynch, John Carpenter, Martin Brest, George Miller, Martha Coolidge, Joel Coen, and Edward Zwick all studied film in college and/or graduate school. From commercial blockbusters such as *Star Wars* (Lucas), *Jaws* (Spielberg), and *The Godfather* saga (Coppola) to smaller, quirkier films such as *The Comfort of Strangers* (Schrader), *Strange Days* (Bigelow), and *Barton Fink* (Coen), these films reflect the tastes and worldviews of the individuals who directed them, but they also reveal the imprimatur of an educational system that teaches students how to write, direct, and criticize motion pictures.

As students of the American cinema, you now share with these directors the benefits of a systematic approach to film education. Like Francis Coppola or George Lucas, you have studied the techniques of classical Hollywood style as well as some of the important genres and individual films in the American cinema. But like these directors, you may also share the pitfalls of an academic approach to movies. Classical Hollywood style is already the dominant narrative film style in the world; learning its history and techniques in the context of higher education may serve only to further cement its domination, thereby inhibiting other ways of looking at the world through film. Not all film schools teach only Hollywood-style filmmaking; those that do, however, have produced the most commercially successful directors.

Like art schools and conservatories of music, film schools have been accused of promoting uniformity at the expense of innovation. Creating works of film art from an academic background, some critics argue, can lead to repetitive, self-reflective, and ultimately empty movies. Then again, self-reflection and repetition in film may be a respectable artistic goal, just as it has been for other twentieth-century talents in other art forms—James Joyce, Philip Glass, Vladimir Nabokov, and Andy Warhol, to name only a few.

Scorsese, Coppola, Schrader, and Lucas all earned graduate degrees in film; Spielberg studied film as an undergraduate. (He applied to USC's graduate film school but was rejected.) In part as a result of their academic training, and in part because of a new critical appreciation of Hollywood films in the 1960s, the film school generation of directors have tended to suffuse their films with references to movies of the past. On the simplest level, for example, when E.T. watches television in Spielberg's *E.T.: The Extra-Terrestrial*, he sees John Wayne on the screen. And Scorsese has said that the opening scene of *Alice Doesn't Live Here Any More* was explicitly designed to suggest *Gone with the Wind, Duel in the Sun, The Wizard of Oz*, and *Invaders from Mars*, all in one.

In an even more complex string of references and influences, the Italian filmmaker Michelangelo Antonioni made an English-language feature film, *Blow Up*, in 1967. It was about a photographer who becomes increasingly confused by the nature of the reality recorded by his camera. In 1974, Francis Coppola made *The Conversation*, which echoes *Blow Up* (though Coppola maintains that he wrote the script for *The Conversation* before seeing *Blow Up*). Coppola complicated the technical as well as the philosophical subject matter by making the protagonist a sound recordist. Finally, in 1981, Brian De Palma made a film about a sound recordist and titled it *Blow Out*, an appropriate term to describe a film that refers to an earlier film, which refers to still an earlier film, which is itself about the problems of recording, understanding, and connecting with the world.

Allusion, quotation, *pastiche*, and *parody*—these are some of the thematic and stylistic hallmarks of the film school generation. In this way, these directors may be understood in terms of *postmodernism*, a cultural phenomenon that spans the arts from architecture to MTV. Broadly defined, postmodernism is an artistic style that seeks both to appropriate and dismantle the conventions of earlier periods. In architecture, for instance, a postmodernist might design a building that has neoclassical columns supporting a modern streamline roof. In music, a postmodern composer might include classically inspired arias in a harsh contemporary opera about terrorists. Seen in the light of postmodernism, then, the film school generation's adaptation of classical Hollywood references toward their own ends is part of a much wider cultural phenomenon of the late 20th century.

Historically, the cinema emerged at roughly the same time as *modernism* in art and literature. In the first quarter of the twentieth century, the work of novelists such as James Joyce and Virginia Woolf and painters such as Pablo Picasso and Marcel Duchamp reflected certain ideas, attitudes, and emotional states particular to the modern era—psychological streams of consciousness, fragmentation of time and space, accelerated motion, technology, urbanization, and so on—with the goal of producing in the reader's or spectator's consciousness a new reality. Film, with its ability to shift perspective by editing and camera movement, thus began as a modernist art form in that it creates in the viewer's mind a consciousness that could not exist otherwise.

In contrast, postmodern artists, composers, and architects—Frank Gehry, Philip Glass, and Vincent Desiderio, to name only a few—have attempted to take this modernist consciousness and break it apart through elaborately, sometimes even glacially intellectual means. To use a favorite postmodern term, they *deconstruct* not only the world they explore through art but the art itself, not to mention the consciousness of the listener, reader, or spectator.

In much the same way, when film school directors draw on their favorite Hollywood films to provide additional layers of meaning, they appropriate the past and put it to new and sometimes opposing uses. For instance, certain directors have repeatedly quoted visual and thematic elements from John Ford's Western *The Searchers*. In George Lucas's *Star Wars*, the burning of

Luke Skywalker's family's homestead is staged to resemble a similar scene in *The Searchers*, and viewers (at least some of whom are presumed to be familiar with *The Searchers*) are invited to enjoy the quotation for its own sake as well as for the sake of the frontier echoes it generates.

Paul Schrader's *Hardcore* is a more complex reworking of *The Searchers*. In Ford's Western, two white men embark on a quest to retrieve a young white woman kidnapped by the Comanche only to find that she may not want to leave her adopted culture. In *Hardcore*, a puritanical father from Michigan tries to rescue his daughter from a life of wild, illicit sex in Southern California, only to find that she rather enjoys it and does not want to return to the Midwest.

Postmodernism is an artistic temperament that uses historical styles and figures in a playful, satirical, often purely decorative manner, thus stripping them of their original context and obscuring their new purpose and meaning. In the context of postmodernism, the kind of expressive, emotional meaning generated by classical Hollywood techniques has given way to a more disjointed intellectual meaning as the film school generation puts the devices of old Hollywood—the techniques used to draw audiences into characters' lives—to precisely the opposite effect. Whereas once these devices brought audiences closer to characters by enhancing identification, they may now serve to distance viewers ironically from the characters on the screen.

For example, think of Robert Zemeckis' *Who Framed Roger Rabbit?* Blending live action and animation in the same shots is not a new, postmodern invention; Walt Disney's *Song of the South* (1946) and *Mary Poppins* (1964) achieved similar effects. But the Disney films are not as self-conscious as *Roger Rabbit*, nor do they appropriate earlier genre conventions and put them to new uses. For instance, Jessica Rabbit is the conventional blonde film noir bombshell, yet she is a "'toon." Moreover, in a new twist on postmodernism's obsession with nostalgia, actual cartoon characters from the past appear—as themselves!—in *Roger Rabbit*, all in the supposedly behind-the-scenes context of a film studio's contract players.

To cite another fairly extreme example, Joel Coen's *Barton Fink* follows the conventions of Hollywood narration to the extent that the male protagonist joins up with an attractive young woman on the beach in the final shot. However, the shot is a precise re-creation of a painting seen earlier in the film on the protagonist's shabby bedroom wall. Coen's "happy ending" is thus contradicted by the fact that it is expressly artificial, a revelation of madness. To top it off, Coen's bright and sunny final shot is further disrupted when, in the final moments, a sea gull flies into the image, appears to have a heart attack in midair, and falls dead into the sea behind the happy couple. The film school generation certainly did not invent ironic distance in Hollywood cinema, but before these directors arrived on the scene such irony would not have been nearly as drastic.

II. SCREENINGS

The suggested screenings for this unit focus on five of the most interesting and successful contemporary American directors—Martin Scorsese, Francis Coppola, Paul Schrader, Steven Spielberg, and Brian De Palma. The individual films have been selected to provide a sampling of each director's artistic range. Remember, they are only suggestions; see *any* film you wish, not only by these directors but by any of the film school directors noted in the program and textbook.

Martin Scorsese:
Taxi Driver (1976)
New York, New York (1977)
Raging Bull (1980)
Goodfellas (1990)
Cape Fear (1991)
The Age of Innocence (1993)
Kundun (1997)
Gangs of New York (2002)
The Aviator (2004)

Francis Ford Coppola:
The Godfather (1972)
The Conversation (1974)
The Godfather, Part II (1974)
Peggy Sue Got Married (1986)
Tucker: The Man and His Dream (1988)
Dracula (1992)
The Rainmaker (1997)

Paul Schrader:
Blue Collar (1978)
Hardcore (1979)
Cat People (1982)
Patty Hearst (1988)
The Comfort of Strangers (1990)
Affliction (1997)
Auto Focus (2002)

Steven Spielberg:
The Sugarland Express (1974)
Jaws (1975)
E.T.: The Extra-Terrestrial (1982)
Empire of the Sun (1987)
Jurassic Park (1993)

Schindler's List (1993)
Saving Private Ryan (1998)
Catch Me If You Can (2002)
The Terminal (2004)

Brian De Palma:
Sisters (1973)
Carrie (1976)
Blow Out (1981)
Scarface (1983)
Raising Cain (1992)
Carlito's Way (1993)
Mission: Impossible (1996)

III. STUDY PLAN FOR THIS UNIT

Getting Started

1. Read Chapter 14: "The 1960s: The Counterculture Strikes Back" and Chapter 15: "The Film School Generation" in *American Cinema/American Culture*.

2. Look through your own college or university catalogue to see what is offered in the way of film courses—film and video production classes, classes in film history and theory, communications classes, and so on. This may give you a sense of the general educational background these directors bring to their work, but as an added benefit, the catalogue may also encourage you to take another film course.

3. Select one of the films listed above—or any film by any of the directors discussed here or in Chapter 15 of the textbook. Because these films are relatively recent, you may have seen a few of them already. Don't just rely on your memory, though; see it again—or, better, see one you don't know anything about.

Watching

1. As you watch the film, note any impressions you may have, and ask yourself these questions:
   - Can I draw any parallels between this film and any earlier films I have seen? Think in terms of genre, character development, and stylistic devices.

- In what ways does the film contrast with earlier films? Consider the sound track, character types, dialogue, theme, and ironic distance.
- Am I able to pick up any quotations from earlier films? (If you do not see any, don't be surprised; the film you have selected simply may not contain any direct film quotes.)

2. As always, write down some of the main ideas raised by the telecourse program as they occur. Be sure to note:
   - who the film school generation includes;
   - why these directors achieved prominence at roughly the same time;
   - how the economics of the film industry played a role in the rise of the movie brats.

3. If any film clips attract your interest, write the title and a brief description in your notes.

For Further Study

1. How were your expectations about the film school generation challenged?

2. What questions and issues could you develop further? Which films did you find most appealing, and could any of them serve as the subject of a research paper or a close analysis?

3. See what it takes to get a degree in film. On the internet, locate the Web sites of one or more of the major film schools, and explore the course offerings and requirements of the film production program.

IV. MEET THE EXPERTS

Peter Bart is editor-in-chief of *Variety*; he is a former Paramount Pictures executive, and the author of *Fade Out: The Calamitous Final Days of M-G-M*.

Peter Biskind is the author of *Easy Riders: The Rise and Fall of the New Hollywood* and *Down and Dirty Pictures: Miramax, Sundance, and the Rise of Independent Film*.

David Brown produced *The Sugarland Express*, *Jaws*, *The Verdict*, and *Cocoon*, among others.

Brian De Palma is the director of *Carrie*, *Obsession*, *Sisters*, *The Fury*, *Body Double*, *Mission: Impossible*, and other films.

Buzz Feitshans produced such films as *Hardcore*, *Big Wednesday*, *Conan the Barbarian*, and *Rambo: First Blood*.

Gray Frederickson is a film producer whose credits include *Apocalypse Now* and *The Godfather, Part III.*

Teri Garr has appeared in such films as *The Conversation, Close Encounters of the Third Kind*, and *After Hours.*

Paul Hirsch edited such films as *Blow Out, The Empire Strikes Back*, and *Mission: Impossible.*

Gary Kurtz produced *American Graffiti* and *Star Wars.*

George Lucas directed *American Graffiti* and went on to change the nature of American filmmaking with his immensely successful *Star Wars* trilogy.

John Milius wrote the screenplays for *The Life and Times of Judge Roy Bean* and *Apocalypse Now*; he wrote and directed *Big Wednesday, Conan the Barbarian*, and *Red Dawn.*

Walter Murch is a sound designer and editor whose credits include *The Conversation, Apocalypse Now, Cold Mountain*, and *The Talented Mr. Ripley.*

Fred Roos is a producer whose credits include Francis Coppola's *The Godfather, Parts II and III, Apocalypse Now*, and *Gardens of Stone.*

Albert Ruddy produced *The Godfather.*

Martin Scorsese is the director of *Boxcar Bertha, The King of Comedy, Alice Doesn't Live Here Any More*, and *After Hours*, as well as some better-known films.

Jonathan Taplin is a film producer whose credits include Martin Scorsese's *Mean Streets* and *The Last Waltz.*

Richard Zanuck is the Oscar-winning film producer responsible for *The Sugarland Express, Jaws*, and *Driving Miss Daisy*, among other films.

V. SUGGESTED READINGS

Biskind, Peter. *Easy Riders, Raging Bulls: How the Sex-Drugs-and-Rock 'n Roll Generation Saved Hollywood.* New York: Simon and Schuster, 1998. A juicy look at the directors, producers, and screenwriters of the film school generation.

Carroll, Noel. "The Future of Allusion: Hollywood in the Seventies (and Beyond)," *October 20* (Spring 1982): 51-81. An essay examining Hollywood's interest in references to films of the past.

MacKinnon, Kenneth. *Misogyny in the Movies: The De Palma Question.* Newark: University of Delaware Press, 1990. A critical analysis of the treatment of women in Brian De Palma's work, concluding that De Palma has not been simplistically misogynistic.

Pye, Michael, and Lynda Myles. *The Movie Brats: How the Film Generation Took Over Hollywood*. New York: Holt, Rinehart and Winston, 1979. An overview of the brats' lives and work.

Thompson, David, and Ian Christie, eds. *Scorsese on Scorsese*. Boston: Faber & Faber, 1990. A book-length, critically annotated series of interviews with Martin Scorsese, who describes his life, working methods, and artistic influences.

Von Gunden, Kenneth. *Postmodern Auteurs: Coppola, Lucas, De Palma, Spielberg, and Scorsese*. Jefferson, NC: McFarland, 1991. A critical examination of the five directors.

VI. EXERCISES AND ASSIGNMENTS

1. The word "postmodernism" has achieved unusually wide usage to describe various elements of contemporary culture. Research postmodernism; explain what it means, and why it is important. Your textbook and this study guide offer definitions of the term. Find others. See what cultural critics have to say about it. Cite examples of postmodernism in other art forms. You may record your work in the form of a written essay, or you may choose to prepare a visual essay in the form of a scrapbook, with pictures and clippings illustrating your findings.

2. Select a sequence from one of the films listed above in the screenings section and analyze it for style and content, concentrating particularly on the ways it conforms or fails to conform to the textbook's and study guide's ideas about the film school generation, parody, pastiche, nostalgia, and so on. Do not hesitate to argue with these ideas.

3. The textbook's discussion of the film school generation begins by citing the influence of the so-called French New Wave directors—Jean-Luc Godard, François Truffaut, and others. Although this is a course on American film history, feel free to expand your awareness of world cinema by researching and screening a film by one of these directors. (Many are available on DVD and VHS.) Write a 5–7 page paper comparing it stylistically to the Hollywood films you have seen. In what ways does it resemble Hollywood films? How is it different?

4. The textbook's discussion of postmodernism and the film school generation focuses in part on a theoretical argument proposed by literary and cultural critic Fredric Jameson. Find Jameson's essay on postmodernism, and critique it in the form of a 5–7 page paper. If you cannot

find this particular essay in your library, you may be able to find either another cultural analysis by Frederic Jameson or another theoretical essay on postmodernism. (Part of the task of this assignment, the most challenging one on this unit, is to define your own goals.) On what political basis does the critic approach postmodernism? Does he or she find postmodernism to be a positive, negative, or value-neutral cultural phenomenon? Once again, do not hesitate to argue with the critic in question. Just be sure to be fair and accurate when explaining his or her argument.

VII. SELF TEST

1. Define or identify the following:
   (a) postmodernism
   (b) Roger Corman
   (c) Brian De Palma
   (d) *auteur*
   (e) *Taxi Driver*
   (f) the French New Wave
   (g) pastiche
   (h) Frederic Jameson

2. Which of the following makes this statement false? Strategies once used to market exploitation films were adopted to sell big-budget films in the 1970s because:
   (a) the films themselves were modeled on genres such as the sci-fi film and the horror film that had formed the backbone of the exploitation market in the 1950s.
   (b) women and minorities were still being exploited in Hollywood films, and audiences had not yet become educated about the damaging consequences of exploitation.
   (c) the cost of producing over 800 prints of each film was offset by the fact that box-office returns could be more than three times higher.
   (d) film audiences were getting older on average, and these aging baby boomers were attracted to films that reminded them of their youth.

3. Short answer: In terms of its cultural meaning, what does the time-travel motif found in certain recent films suggest?

4. True or false:
   (a) When critic Robin Wood describes *Taxi Driver* as an "incoherent text," he means that the film is poorly made and full of meaningless violence.
   (b) Directors of the film school generation tended to disregard the aesthetics of American directors of the past and preferred instead to emulate Jean-Luc Godard, François Truffaut, and other French directors.
   (c) One of the most notable aspects of films made by the movie brats is that many were written by young film critics who put their critical tastes and sensibilities to practical use.
   (d) The greatest increase in university film school courses occurred in the early 1960s and was sparked by the influence of such commercial hits as Alfred Hitchcock's *Psycho* and John Ford's *The Searchers*.

5. Essay: What is postmodernism, and what does it have to do with the movie brats?

INTO THE 21ST CENTURY

I. INTO THE 21ST CENTURY: AN OVERVIEW

In the Declaration of Independence, Thomas Jefferson held certain truths to be self-evident, among them the people's right to form a new government whenever an existing one fails to protect life, ensure liberty, and encourage the pursuit of happiness. In American filmmaking, strangely enough, independence is much less clearly defined, let alone maintained. Owing in part to the extraordinary film technology, vast staffs, and expansive facilities available to Hollywood directors, and even more to the tantalizing power of money, today's independent filmmaker may well turn into the Hollywood dealmaker of tomorrow. Must he or she necessarily forfeit life, liberty, and happiness in the process?

This unit covers two related issues: recent Hollywood cinema and American independent filmmakers of the last twenty years. (Note: *American Cinema/American Culture* covers the former, the telecourse program *The Edge of Hollywood* covers the latter.) These questions begin and end with two of the murkiest questions in practical film criticism. What does independence really mean in the American film industry? And given Hollywood's power and influence, are American directors ever able to remain independent?

For some filmgoers, the idea of an American independent cinema is itself reassuring, no matter how these films compare qualitatively with Hollywood's. For others, particularly minority and feminist audiences, independent film production provides a vital alternative to the mostly white, generally male-oriented, almost exclusively heterosexual myths sustained by Hollywood. Women like Kathryn Bigelow, Nancy Savoca, and Penelope Spheeris; African-Americans like Spike Lee and Carl Franklin; Asian-Americans like Wayne Wang; and openly gay men like Gus Van Sant, Greg Araki, and John Waters—all are important role models as directors. Their backgrounds and sensibilities may have produced alternative ways of looking at the world through film, and they all got their start as independents.

Does independence necessarily involve an alternative, possibly radical point of view in addition to financing and production outside of Hollywood studios? One way film reviewers often define independence is by judging the filmmaker's artistic vision. In this way, an independent filmmaker is one whose films seem offbeat and unusual. Thus, some critics see David Lynch, who directed the unconventional-seeming *Blue Velvet*, as an independent director, whereas Francis Coppola tends to be viewed as a typical Hollywood player. Similarly, Spike Lee, who made *Malcolm X* and *Do the Right Thing*, is generally seen as an independent director, whereas Steven Spielberg is not.

This method of categorizing directors may seem to have the force of common sense on its side. After all, one of the virtues of independent cinema is that it is able to operate out of the artistic mainstream to produce films that look and sound different than the films screened at the average suburban octoplex. However, this definition of cinematic independence is based on an essentially romantic notion of artistic freedom that does not take into account the central problem of independent filmmaking—namely, *financing*. Lynch's *Blue Velvet* may seem more offbeat than, say, the gargantuan 1970s remake of *King Kong*, but, in fact, both were financed by longtime Hollywood producer Dino De Laurentiis. *Do the Right Thing* may appear to be more politically unconventional than, say, *Back to the Future, Part II* or *Uncle Buck*, but all three were produced by Universal Pictures. And although he has directed many films in Hollywood, Francis Coppola was so concerned about maintaining his artistic independence that he founded his own studio, Zoetrope. Of these three filmmakers, one is no more independent than the others.

For any director, making a film means finding the money to pay for it. As a result, true independence has always been nearly impossible, since most filmmakers are not multimillionaires when they begin making films. Once they achieve commercial success, they often form their own companies and work in tandem with studios. This financial tension began early in American film history. In the 1900s and early 1910s, the Motion Picture Patents Company monopolized film production by controlling patents on equipment and by attempting to license production and distribution of films. Rebelling against this monopolistic control, two producers, William Fox and Carl Laemmle, began making films outside of the Motion Picture Patents Company's vast sphere of influence and thus became two of the earliest American independent filmmakers. However, neither Fox nor Laemmle remained "independent"; Fox's company evolved into 20th Century-Fox, while Laemmle's became Universal Pictures.

Hollywood has always been attractive to filmmakers precisely because the system offered the necessary capital. During the studio era, when vertical integration and a consistent mass audience helped to ensure a steady flow of cash, many European directors were enticed by the studios to abandon their national cinemas and move to Hollywood, where they were given lucrative contracts and a dazzling array of expensive cameras, lights, actors, and special-effects equipment to play with. This lure still holds its power over contemporary American directors as well, for while the studios no longer have the corporate stability they once did, they nevertheless maintain the financial and technical means to make big-budget motion pictures. In the United States, these resources are denied to independent filmmakers.

David Lynch, for instance, would not likely have had the resources to create *Blue Velvet* without the backing of a seasoned Hollywood producer like Dino De Laurentiis. Spike Lee, too, would probably have had to spend several years simply piecing together the financing for *Do the Right Thing*, just as he spent a considerable amount of time and energy in preproduction for his earlier feature, *She's Gotta Have It*. Lee has called his earlier beg-borrow-and-steal approach "guerilla filmmaking"—an appropriate term, given the desperate lengths to which independent filmmakers are driven to see their films through to completion. Small public arts grants, foundation grants, private contributions by individuals, discounts and outright donations by film editing facilities and processing laboratories, and even bartering with other filmmakers—this is the piecemeal financing system to which American independent filmmakers are unfortunately all too closely bound. On a more positive note, independent filmmakers are given support by such training grounds and exhibition venues as Robert Redford's Sundance Institute, where writers and directors receive practical filmmaking education, and the Telluride Film Festival, where their work is shown to distributors and film executives looking to make the next big talent discovery.

Hollywood may place artistic constraints on its directors, but it enables filmmakers to work on a far more elaborate scale than would be possible if they remained truly independent. As a result, many top American independent filmmakers have risen to prominence outside of Hollywood only to strike studio deals on the basis of their independent successes—deals that bring with them bigger budgets and higher production values. For example, Joel and Ethan Coen made *Blood Simple* as an independent feature in 1984; less than a decade later they were making a $30 million film, *The Hudsucker Proxy*, for producer Joel Silver, whose action-adventure films (*Lethal Weapon*, *Die Hard*, *The Matrix*, and so on) epitomize contemporary Hollywood megabudget moviemaking. The Coen brothers continue to make films which to all appearances exist outside the Hollywood mainstream. But how can they continue to be independent filmmakers once they have been hired by Joel Silver?

Despite its unanswerable nature, the question of filmmaking independence is worth pursuing if only to gain a familiarity with a group of filmmakers whose works stand somewhat outside the mainstream of Hollywood taste and sensibility. In the last 30 years, the American cinema has produced a number of talented directors who have managed to make films outside of the Hollywood system, films that themselves tend to challenge Hollywood norms both aesthetically and sociologically. Robert Altman, John Cassavetes, John Sayles, George Romero, John Waters, Wayne Wang, Spike Lee, Penelope Spheeris, Gus Van Sant, Joel and Ethan Coen, Kathryn Bigelow, and David Lynch are some of the most notable directors in this regard. In broad terms, they fall into two categories—those who have worked in Hollywood often, and those who have not. For the purposes of this unit, they are all treated as independent filmmakers to the extent that they have made feature films outside of Hollywood at one point or another in their careers.

Most of these directors, like Kathryn Bigelow and John Waters to cite only two, progressed from making small, independent features to directing bigger budget Hollywood films. Bigelow's first feature, *The Loveless*, was independently produced; she went on to direct Harrison Ford in *K-19: The Widowmaker*. Waters began with a string of hilarious, defiantly offensive films made in Baltimore in the 1970s. Featuring a 300-pound drag queen named Divine, Waters' films are a sustained celebration of precisely the kind of bad taste and intense vulgarity Hollywood films cannot ever hope to achieve. As such, they became instant cult classics. By 1990, Waters had gone on to make *Cry Baby* with Johnny Depp. Waters' vision was still independent, though not nearly as raunchy; his financing however was pure Hollywood.

Other directors, such as John Sayles and John Cassavetes, generally managed to steer clear of Hollywood deals, at least as far as directing contracts are concerned. Cassavetes worked frequently as an actor in Hollywood films (*Rosemary's Baby, The Fury, The Dirty Dozen*). Through this route, he managed to earn enough money to pay for his own independent features—dynamic, character-oriented films about race (*Shadows*), gender politics and insanity (*A Woman Under the Influence*), and other less easily pigeonholed subjects (*Gloria, Husbands, Faces,* and others).

Sayles, the director of such films as *The Return of the Secaucus Seven, Lianna,* and *City of Hope*, began his filmmaking career in Hollywood working as a screenwriter (*Piranha, The Lady in Red,* and others) for producer Roger Corman. *The Return of the Secaucus Seven* was his first film as a director; a genuinely independent production, it was shot in four weeks on a budget of $40,000. Sayles has continued to make independently financed films that reflect his own humanistic vision, including *Lianna*, a lesbian coming-out story; *Matewan*, a film about a labor dispute in West Virginia; *Eight Men Out*, a complex morality story about the 1919 baseball team that threw the World Series; and *Sunshine State*, a drama about land deals in Florida.

In terms of artistic and commercial influence, George Romero's success as an independent director remains oddly undervalued, perhaps because his low-budget horror films have tended to play better with audiences than with film reviewers. The Pittsburgh-based Romero's first feature, *Night of the Living Dead*, was made with local actors and crew on a budget of $70,000. A graphic, shockingly realistic tale of zombies who live on human flesh, the film achieved extraordinary success on the midnight-movie circuit in the late 1960s and early 1970s. *Night of the Living Dead* paved the way for other independently produced midnight movies such as David Lynch's *Eraserhead* and John Waters *Pink Flamingoes*, and it ushered in a host of other *splatter films*—a term that accurately describes the gory special effects that characterize not only Romero's films but also such 1970s and 1980s Hollywood staples as the *Friday the 13th, Halloween,* and *Nightmare on Elm Street* series. In this way, Romero's unconventionally explicit blood-and-guts brand of horror, made possible by his independence from Hollywood codes of cinematic conduct, nevertheless became one of Hollywood's most consistent conventions.

As a concept, independent filmmaking has a nice ring to it, but in contemporary American cinema the idea is more feasible than the reality. Penelope Spheeris provides an interesting case in point in terms of the difficulty—if not outright futility—of analyzing contemporary filmmakers' work solely in terms of independence from Hollywood. In the 1980s, Spheeris directed several independent, low-budget films about disaffected youth (*The Decline of Western Civilization* and *Suburbia*, to name two). As a result, she became something of a cult figure on the fringes of the punk and heavy metal worlds—a female director breaking the double gender barriers of music and filmmaking. In 1991, Spheeris was hired by Paramount Pictures to direct *Wayne's World*, which was released in 1992 much to many reviewers' dismay. On closer inspection, the hugely profitable, vastly underrated *Wayne's World* defies certain Hollywood conventions and parodies others. (At one point, for instance Spheeris' camera turns away from Wayne and begins to track with a minor character; Wayne yells at the camera, which responds by conforming to convention once again—it learns to concern itself solely with the central character in pursuit of his goals.) In this way, *Wayne's World* may be every bit as independent in its vision as *Suburbia*, Paramount's box-office receipts for the later film notwithstanding. Few critics would characterize *Wayne's World* as independent, however, and they would be correct: films made by Hollywood studios are not independent, no matter how unconventional they may be.

II. SCREENINGS

Here is a selective list of independent filmmakers and their best and/or most representative works. As you are learning in this unit, independence from Hollywood is more accurately defined film by film rather than filmmaker by filmmaker. For instance, some of Robert Altman's best films (*M*A*S*H* and *Nashville*, for instance) were produced and distributed by studios. Consequently, you may choose to see either a studio film by an independent-minded director (Waters' *Hairspray*, for example) or an independently produced film by someone like Cassavetes, Sayles, or Romero.

Robert Altman:
   *M*A*S*H* (1970)
   Nashville (1975)
   Come Back to the 5 & Dime Jimmy Dean, Jimmy Dean (1982)
   The Player (1992)
   Gosford Park (2001)
   The Company (2003)

Kathryn Bigelow:
   The Loveless (1981)

Near Dark (1987)
Blue Steel (1989)
Strange Days (1995)
K-19: The Widowmaker (2002)

John Cassavetes:
Shadows (1960)
Faces (1968)
Husbands (1970)
A Woman Under the Influence (1974)
Gloria (1980)

Spike Lee:
She's Gotta Have It (1986)
School Daze (1988)
Do the Right Thing (1989)
Mo' Better Blues (1990)
Malcolm X (1992)
Summer of Sam (1999)
She Hate Me (2004)

David Lynch:
Eraserhead (1977)
Blue Velvet (1986)
Wild at Heart (1990)
Lost Highway (1997)
Mulholland Dr. (2001)

George Romero:
Night of the Living Dead (1968)
Martin (1978)
Dawn of the Dead (1979)
Day of the Dead (1985)
Monkey Shines (1988)

Gus Van Sant:
Mala Noche (1985)
Drugstore Cowboy (1989)
My Own Private Idaho (1991)
To Die For (1995)
Good Will Hunting (1997)
Elephant (2003)

John Sayles:
The Return of the Secaucus Seven (1979)

Lianna (1982)
Matewan (1987)
Eight Men Out (1988)
City of Hope (1991)
Lone Star (1996)
Sunshine State (2002)

Penelope Spheeris:
The Decline of Western Civilization (1980)
Suburbia (aka *The Wild Side*, 1983)
The Decline of Western Civilization, Part II (1988)
Wayne's World (1992)

John Waters:
Pink Flamingoes (1972)
Female Trouble (1975)
Desperate Living (1977)
Polyester (1981)
Hairspray (1988)
Cry-Baby (1990)
Pecker (1998)
A Dirty Shame (2004)

III. STUDY PLAN FOR THIS UNIT

Getting Started

1. Read Chapter 16: "Into the Twenty-First Century," in *American Cinema/ American Culture.*

2. Take the time to screen at least one of the films listed above, an independent film of your choice, or a recent Hollywood film you haven't already seen. Here are some tips on selecting a film:
   (a) Because some of the films listed above are small, independent productions, and because some of them are rarely screened in college film courses, you may have trouble locating them in your college library. Some will be available in a well-stocked video store, but be prepared—take a list of second and third choices.
   (b) As alternative visions, some of these films may shock you. This is not necessarily a reason to avoid seeing them, but proceed at your own risk.

(c) Don't hesitate to ask for advice at your local video store for recent independent films.

Watching

1. As you watch the film, and immediately after it's over, take some notes about the main ideas it raises as well as elements of its style.

2. If you are assigned to watch the telecourse program "Into the 21st Century," take notes on things such as:
   - who "the independents" are, and what makes them independent;
   - the economics of contemporary independent film production;
   - the role genre films have played in American independent cinema;
   - how independents both embrace and challenge films of the past.

3. As always, be on the lookout for any film clips that interest you. Make a note of them in case you decide to research the film further.

For Further Study

1. Fill in any gaps in your notes.

2. Were there any points raised in the telecourse program that you thought were incorrect? Did any of the experts say things that you found to be problematic? By all means: take your negative responses as seriously as your positive ones. Ask your instructor what he or she thinks about the issues.

3. Ask yourself:
   - How were my expectations about American independent cinema met by the film I saw? Did I discover that I was already familiar with what I experienced?
   - How were my expectations confronted and challenged? Did the film change the way I think about low-budget movies, for instance? About film conventions? About minority issues in contemporary American films?
   - How does the telecourse program compare with others in the series? Was the topic clear? Did the filmmakers address issues that were important to me?
   - On the basis of this program, am I able to define what makes an American director independent? Have I gained any sense of film history from this program?

IV. MEET THE EXPERTS

Gregg Araki directed *Mysterious Skin, Totally F***ed Up,* and *The Living End,* a road movie about two HIV-positive gay men.

Ethan Coen is the producer and coscreenwriter of *Blood Simple, Raising Arizona, Miller's Crossing, Barton Fink, The Hudsucker Proxy,* and *Fargo,* among other films.

Joel Coen directed and cowrote *Blood Simple, Raising Arizona, Miller's Crossing, Barton Fink,* and *The Hudsucker Proxy,* and *Fargo,* among other films.

Julie Dash directed *Illusions,* the story of an African-American Hollywood executive passing for white in the 1940s, and *Daughters in the Dust,* about the women of the Sea Islands, off the southern Atlantic coast.

Carl Franklin is the director of *One False Move, Nowhere to Run,* and *Out of Time,* among other films.

Nick Gomez, **Bob Gosse**, and **Larry Meistrich** run The Shooting Gallery, a production facility for independent filmmakers.

J. Hoberman, a film critic for the *Village Voice,* is the author of *Vulgar Modernism* and *Bridge of Light: Yiddish Film Between Two Worlds*; he is also the coauthor of *Midnight Movies.*

Richard Jameson was the editor of *Film Comment* magazine.

Jim Jarmusch directed *Stranger Than Paradise, Down by Law, Mystery Train, Night on Earth, Dead Man,* and *Ghost Dog: The Way of the Samurai.*

Tom Kalin directed the independent film *Swoon,* about the notorious Leopold and Loeb murder trial.

Harvey Keitel has appeared in many American and European films, such as *Mean Streets, Taxi Driver, Thelma and Louise, La Nuit de Varennes,* and *Bad Timing.*

Todd McCarthy has written film criticism for *Variety, Film Comment, American Film,* and *Positif* and is the co-director of *Visions of Light.*

Larry Meistrich is the producer of *Laws of Gravity.*

John Pierson produced Spike Lee's *She's Gotta Have It.*

Sam Raimi has directed stylized horror films such as *The Evil Dead, Darkman, Spider-Man,* and *Spider-Man 2.*

Joel Silver produced such films as *The Matrix,* Lethal *Weapon, Die Hard,* and *The Hudsucker Proxy.*

Steven Soderbergh directed *sex, lies, and videotape, Traffic, Erin Brockovich,* and *Ocean's Eleven,* among other films.

Jim Stark is a film producer whose credits include Jim Jarmusch's *Stranger than Paradise*, *Down By Law*, and *Night on Earth*.

Quentin Tarantino directed *Reservoir Dogs*, *Pulp Fiction*, and *Kill Bill*.

John Turturro has appeared in such films as *Do the Right Thing*, *Five Corners*, *Barton Fink*, *She Hate Me*, and *O Brother, Where Art Thou?*.

Christine Vachon produced *Swoon*, *One Hour Photo*, *Far From Heaven*, and many other films.

V. SUGGESTED READINGS

Biskind, Peter. *Down and Dirty Pictures: Miramax, Sundance, and the Rise of Independent Film*. New York: Simon and Schuster, 2004. A look at how the ideals of independent filmmaking have met the reality of corporate financing, influence, and hype.

Carney, Raymond. *American Dreaming: The Films of John Cassavetes and the American Experience*. Berkeley: University of California Press, 1985. A critical survey of Cassavetes's career and his cinematic vision of American culture.

Hoberman, J., and Jonathan Rosenbaum. *Midnight Movies*. New York: Harper & Row, 1983. A perceptive, articulate, and appreciative survey of popular, independently produced cult films such as *Multiple Maniacs*, *Night of the Living Dead*, and *Glen or Glenda: I Changed My Sex*.

Keyssar, Helene. *Robert Altman's America*. New York: Oxford University Press, 1991. An auteurist survey of some of Altman's films.

MacDonald, Scott. *A Critical Cinema: Interviews with Independent Filmmakers*. Berkeley: University of California Press, 1988. Interviews with various independent filmmakers, including George Kuchar, Hollis Frampton, Beth B. and Scott B., and John Waters.

McGilligan, Patrick. *Robert Altman: Jumping Off the Cliff*. New York: St. Martin's Press, 1989. A critical biography of the director.

McMillan, Terry. *Five for Five: The Films of Spike Lee*. New York: Stewart, Tabori, and Chang, 1991. A series of essays on Lee's feature films.

VI. EXERCISES AND ASSIGNMENTS

1. Now that you are reaching the end of this course, you should be able to begin reviewing films from an informed point of view. If you have been assigned the telecourse program "The Independents," write a brief review of it. Compare it to some of the other programs you have seen throughout the course, or to any other documentaries you have seen. Critique the program on the basis of both style and content. Have the filmmakers presented their ideas clearly? Do not hesitate to attack the program if you choose, but remember: support your criticisms with hard evidence in the form of concrete details and observations.

2. This unit offers a particularly good opportunity for you to explore issues of ethnicity, race, gender, and sexual orientation by researching independent minority filmmakers of the past and present. Use the telecourse program and textbook chapter as preliminary guides, but don't stop there. Find out more about independent directors who speak directly to your concerns. Ask your librarian to help you find current newspapers and magazines aimed at specific ethnic, racial, or sexual groups. In them, you may find reviews of independent films you would otherwise never hear about.

3. Many magazines, both online and in print, cover the current independent filmmaking scene. So give yourself an independent research assignment: find one of these journals, read through several issues, select a topic of interest and write a 3-5 page paper on it. This assignment reflects one of the problems faced by independent filmmakers—namely, maintaining motivation without either structure or the promise of certain success. As a general guide, bear in mind that your topic may be biographical (the life and career of a contemporary filmmaker), economic (a current issue in independent film financing), technological (new developments in film equipment that facilitate small, independent productions), or any category that strikes your interest.

4. Explore the work of an individual filmmaker in detail by closely analyzing a sequence from his or her work. This exercise is especially appropriate in this unit, since a close analysis will enable you to judge the extent to which the filmmaker in question is *stylistically* independent. In what ways does the filmmaker use the techniques of classical Hollywood style? Does the filmmaker violate those principles in any way?

VII. SELF TEST

1. Define or identify the following:
   (a) guerilla filmmaking
   (b) John Cassavetes
   (c) splatter films
   (d) Joel Coen
   (e) *The Return of the Secaucus Seven*
   (f) Zoetrope Studios
   (g) Robert Altman
   (h) Divine

2. Which of the following makes this statement false? Independent film production in the United States:
   (a) began in the late 1960s, when film school graduates began making films outside the studio system.
   (b) began in the late 1970s, when women and African-Americans first appeared on the filmmaking horizon.
   (c) was given a boost in the early 1910s by two producers, Carl Laemmle and William Fox, who challenged a powerful monopoly's control on filmmaking.
   (d) has been practiced by such directors as John Waters, George Romero, and Francis Coppola.

3. Short answer: According to the directors interviewed in the program, what are some of the major difficulties of independent filmmaking in the United States?

4. True or false:
   (a) David Lynch directed *Blue Velvet*, which was produced by a consortium of small, independent producers with radical ideas about filmmaking.
   (b) Penelope Spheeris directed *Wayne's World* and thus helped Paramount Pictures make a lot of money.
   (c) John Cassavetes had two successful careers—one as an actor in such films as *Rosemary's Baby*, the other as an independent director.
   (d) The Coen brothers have made enough money with their early, studio-financed films that they can now afford to maintain their independence by never working with commercial Hollywood producers.

5. Essay: What makes a director independent? Feel free to critique either the study guide's or the program's definition of independence.

SUPPLEMENTARY UNIT A

Film Language

INTRODUCTION

As the first of the three "supplementary" units in the course, this unit has been designed as an overview of the basic formal and critical language of the motion picture. The terms and concepts outlined here may be applied throughout the course. They comprise the essential vocabulary of formal film criticism, serving as the tools with which films are described in close analyses. In addition, this critical language is also useful when analyzing films from the perspective of cultural studies, for it enables critics, scholars, and students to move beyond generalities about a given film's contents toward concrete details about the nature and meaning of a given image or sequence.

Like the terminology used in biology or chemistry, film terms refer to particular and observable aspects, components, or qualities of the object being studied. In this case, the object is the raw formal material of the movies. Gaining a working knowledge of this terminology will help you not only speak and write more clearly about films but also, more fundamentally, begin to *see* and *hear* the way motion pictures are constructed.

WITHIN THE IMAGE: THE SHOT

If films are expressive works of art, how is their meaning expressed? Imagine an image of a cowboy on the screen. You recognize him as a cowboy because he is wearing a conventional Western outfit and is standing next to a horse. But *how* are you seeing him? Is he close or far away? Is he seen from above, from below, or at eye level? Is his face in shadow or in sunlight? Does the camera move? If so, where? And what images appear before or after the cowboy's? Do these surrounding images add any meaning to the cowboy's image?

You could describe the image on the screen in terms of its relationship to American history and the settling of the West, but unless you knew how to analyze the image in terms of its own characteristics, your description would remain incomplete. The way the image *itself* looks tells you as much about the cowboy as his costume, his speech, or the landscape against which he is photographed.

First, the individual images you see on the screen are called *shots*. The shot is the basic element of a film's construction, a kind of building block from which an entire film is pieced together. A shot is simply a piece of motion picture film that has been exposed in a camera in a single, uninterrupted run. Shots vary in length from a second or even a fraction of a second to several minutes and even longer. Within every shot is a series of *frames*, or individual pictures. If you hold a piece of motion picture film up to a light source, you can see how these frames vary slightly from each other, producing an illusion of movement when the film is run through a projector. Every shot begins and ends with a *transition* linking it to the preceding or following shot; these transitions include the *cut*, the *dissolve*, the *wipe*, and the *fade-in* and *fade-out*. These transitions will be covered later in this overview; for the moment, concentrate only on the shot and the range of expressive qualities contained within it.

One way shots are distinguished and defined is by the apparent distance between the camera and the subject being filmed. The terms used to describe these different kinds of shots are straightforward. A *long shot* is one in which the camera appears to be at a long distance from the subject. (Lenses may create the illusion of great distance when the camera is in fact much closer.) A long shot of the cowboy would include not only the cowboy and his horse but also the ground on which he stands as well as the sky behind him. In other words, long shots reveal not only the subject but also the physical context in which he, she, or it is placed. A *medium shot* of the same cowboy is taken from a somewhat closer position. We might see the horse's head if the horse is standing very near the cowboy, and we would see the cowboy from the waist up. And a *close-up* of the cowboy is taken from a very close position. Close-ups isolate one element in the image, often the human face. In close-ups, the physical context of the subject is limited because the subject itself takes up most of the space on the screen.

Although generalizations in art criticism often prove to be wrong, a certain degree of generality is necessary in defining the conventional expressive qualities of these different types of shots. After all, classical Hollywood style developed as a system of generalities in which the formal elements of the cinema were designed to be understood in similar ways. Conventions of subject-camera distance developed precisely in this manner. Consider, for instance, what you would see and learn about a cowboy in long shot. The details of his face would not be especially clear, but his costume, physical stance, and horse would be, not to mention the landscape around him. You would see his context, but not his individuality, which is most often expressed artistically by way of facial contours and expressions. As a result, Hollywood cinema often uses long shots not only to set a character or object within a physical environment but also to express a kind of emotional distance from the subject.

If you were directing the shot of the cowboy and wanted instead to get a sense of his interior life while still maintaining some exterior context, you might choose to film him in medium shot. A medium shot would contain some of the elements of his costume (not to mention some of his horse), but would also reveal the expression on his face much more clearly than a long shot. If you wanted to give the audience an even stronger impression of the cowboy's emotional state, you would likely choose to film him in close-up, for a close-up would reveal the lines on his face, the expressive shape of his mouth, and perhaps most important of all, the intense emotions revealed by his eyes.

In general in the Hollywood cinema, the closer the camera moves toward a character's face, the more details emerge about his or her emotional state. If the cowboy had dark, squinting eyes and a small scar on his left cheek, for instance, these expressive details, seen in extreme close-up, would reveal something crucial about the character at that moment. He would be the same cowboy seen earlier in long shot, but the audience will likely understand him in a completely different way by virtue of the closeness of the camera.

Shots are also described in terms of the camera's angle in relation to the subject. A *high-angle shot* is taken from above the subject, a *low-angle shot* from below the subject, and an *eye-level* shot is taken straight on. Once again, broad generalizations about the expressive meaning of these different angles are dangerous. Still, a set of expressive conventions did arise and continues to thrive in Hollywood cinema: high-angle shots, because they literally look down on the subject, tend to diminish the subject emotionally, while low-angle shots, like a child's gaze toward a parent, tend to make the subject seem somewhat grander and more heroic. As you begin to see and understand films more closely, you will no doubt find countless exceptions to this tendency. With camera angles, as with everything else, the expressive meaning of a given shot depends not simply on widespread Hollywood conventions but on the formal patterns established within an individual film, a given filmmaker's point of view, the content of the scene, and so on. But for the purposes of this overview, imagine three medium shots of the cowboy: the first in high angle, the second in low angle, and the third from eye level. If you were directing the film, and you wanted to make the cowboy look particularly threatening, which angle would you select? (Most directors would pick a low-angle shot, but remember—there is no correct answer here. It's a question of how you as a director envision your subject and how well you convey your expressive vision to the audience.)

Shots are also defined by their content. Here, the terms are ridiculously simple. A *two-shot* contains two people, either in medium shot or close-up, and a *three-shot* contains three people. Finally, a *master shot* reveals the entire space of the scene including all of the characters. In the case of the cowboy and his horse, a medium shot containing both of them would be called a two-shot, even though one of the characters isn't human.

Consider for a moment the expressive value of such a two-shot. If the director repeatedly filmed the cowboy in a two-shot with his horse, a relationship between the two characters would begin to be formed in the audience's mind because the cowboy and his horse would be seen again and again as an inseparable team—formally as well as dramatically. On the other hand, if the cowboy and his horse were rarely seen together in the same shot, except perhaps for some conventional shots of the cowboy riding away in the distance, a very different relationship between man and horse would be suggested.

Of course, if a two-shot works for a cowboy and his horse, it is not difficult to imagine the expressive value it has in a film about two human beings. An argument, a courtship, a mother-daughter discussion, a growing friendship—any encounter between two people will be given an additional level of meaning by the nature of the shots used to film it. For example, a director might wish to undercut the sentimentality of a love scene by refusing to film the two people in a two-shot. Instead, he or she may prefer to cut back and forth between the characters, separating them in screen space even while they are speaking about being in love. Similarly, a director may enhance the passion underlying a violent argument between two characters by filming them in a two-shot, thereby expressing that these two people are an inseparable team even when they are fighting.

Finally, shots are described by virtue of the camera's movement. Camera movement is one of the most aesthetically pleasing devices in the cinema, for it adds its own motion to the motion of people and things within the image. Camera movement is such an integral part of films and television that it is often taken for granted. But imagine for a moment that cameras could *not* move. Everything would have to occur precisely in front of the camera, and the resulting film would seem stilted and restrictive.

Now imagine that you are suddenly free to move the camera left and right and up and down. The scope of the world you are able to film expands dramatically, as does your range of expression. By rotating the camera horizontally, you create a *panning shot* or *pan*. By rotating it vertically, you create a *tilt*. Pans and tilts are common and effective devices in filmmaking, for they enable the camera to record much more information about the physical space of a scene than would be possible otherwise—a sense of the Grand Canyon's length by panning, for instance, or a skyscraper's height by tilting.

Now imagine that the tripod *itself* is able to move in any direction—forward, backward, sideways, and into the air. In Hollywood's golden age, studio technicians actually laid railroadlike tracks on which cameras could roll back and forth smoothly. For this reason, shots containing forward, backward, or sideways movement of the camera are called *tracking shots*. (They are also called *dolly shots*, after the dolly wheels that provide similar mobility.) Tracking shots can be very expressive, not only because of their graceful formal movement but also because they may dramatically emphasize the subject at hand. Camera movements function as a form of selection within a shot, underscoring the importance of a character or object by moving closer to it.

Think of the cowboy, still standing patiently with his horse. Imagine that the shot in question will be the first shot in the film. Beginning with a long shot of an empty expanse of land, the high plains in Colorado, the camera pans slowly to the right, revealing the openness and seeming endlessness of the West. Finally, in the distance, a man and his horse are revealed. The camera then tracks forward toward the man, first slowly, and then with increasing speed until the camera suddenly stops at the point at which the man and his horse are seen in a two-shot.

What might the various elements of this shot express? In what other ways could the opening of this film have been filmed?

Motion picture cameras are not compelled to stay on the ground. They may be placed on long, swinging, mechanical arms to create *crane shots*. Crane shots often serve as the first shot of a film or scene, smoothly lowering the spectator into the action. They also enable the camera to follow a character smoothly up or down a flight of stairs without the use of cuts, or to peep into a second-floor window, or perform any motion involving shifts in height.

In addition, cameras can move anywhere a human being can move simply by virtue of a camera operator's ability to hold the camera in his or her hands. *Hand-held shots* sometimes have a slightly bumpy, jerky quality. Far from being considered detrimental, these inadvertent wobbles are generally perceived as a convention of realism, implicitly acknowledging the existence of the camera in a subtle but evocative rejection of Hollywood artificiality. However, the force and beauty of Hollywood polish has produced, through technology, the ability to create hand-held shots that are utterly smooth. *Steadicam shots*, taken with a patented device that fits around the camera operator's waist, eliminate the inadvertent bumps and allow the operator to walk, run, or maneuver through rocky ground without disrupting the flow of the shot.

Finally, *zoom* lenses create the impression of movement even though the camera does not in fact move. Zoom shots or zooms are taken with a lens with a variable focal length, shifting in the same shot between wide-angle and long-focus or telephoto. It's important to remember that the terms *zooming* and *tracking* cannot be used interchangeably. Tracking shots move the audience physically in space; zooms "move" the audience's consciousness toward or away from a given object. For example, if a character named Caitlin is searching for her friend Emily in a crowded shopping mall, a zoom forward on Emily would demonstrate a change in Caitlin's consciousness but not in her physical position. The zoom tells the audience that Caitlin has picked Emily out from the crowd without moving herself. In contrast, if the camera tracked forward on Emily, the audience would probably understand that Caitlin had already located Emily and was now actually moving toward her.

Cameras may perform several different types of movement at once. These movements may create not only sweeping, elegant formal figures on the screen but also twisted linguistic problems for the critic and student. In other words, do not be surprised when the graceful camera movements you see onscreen turn out to be difficult to describe on paper. For example: "The camera cranes down, then pans left while simultaneously tracking forward. . . ." To get an immediate sense of this problem, take a short walk around the room, and then describe not only what you have seen *but also the way you have seen it*. It will probably take you much longer to describe your vision of the room than it did to experience the room itself. Similarly, ten seconds of film may be immediately readable in terms of its expressive qualities, but when you try to describe it in words, you may discover that it is a great deal more complicated than it seems.

FROM IMAGE TO IMAGE: EDITING

If shots are like building blocks, how do they fit together? As you have seen, shots contain expressive qualities within themselves, but a further level of expression occurs through the relationships created between shots—in other words, through editing. The most common way of joining shots together is simply to cut and splice them. Not surprisingly, this transition is called a *cut*. In filmmaking, cutting occurs in a literal way: an editor examines a shot frame by frame, decides where to make the cut, then physically snips the film at that point and tapes it to another shot. (Later, in processing, the tape is eliminated and the film is transferred to a single continuous piece of celluloid.)

To see the way in which meaning is created by cutting, imagine that the following shots have been cut together: a close-up of a woman's expressionless face, a close-up of a baby's coffin, a close-up of a woman's hand holding a handkerchief, a close-up of a stuffed animal lying on the ground, a close-up of a bouquet of flowers, and finally another close-up of the woman's expressionless face. How do you read the sequence?

It's likely that you would make certain assumptions not only about the individual shots but about their relationship to each other—in other words, you would tell yourself a story about the woman, her emotions, and her relationship to the coffin and stuffed animal. You might very well assume that the woman is the mother of an infant who has died, that she is mourning the child, and that a funeral is taking place. The editing of the sequence certainly suggests such a narrative. Would it surprise you to learn that the close-up of the woman had been filmed at a hairdresser's shop, the baby's coffin at a funeral supplies warehouse, the woman's hand at an allergist's office, the stuffed animal at a department store, and the flowers at a wedding? More important, *would it matter why and where these shots were originally filmed?* In this instance, the meaning of the shots results at least as much from their relationship to each other as from what they contain individually. Despite the reality of how and why they were originally filmed, their editing tells a story of its own.

Chapter 3: "Classical Hollywood Cinema: Style," in John Belton's *American Cinema/American Culture*, describes in detail the various types of editing used in Hollywood films. For now, consider briefly the two major categories of editing: editing within scenes and editing from scene to scene. The suggestive funeral sequence, above, is an example of editing within an individual scene. Here, a short narrative fragment is created by linking a series of shots together. If the shots were created according to certain principles of lighting and camera placement, a unified (though imaginary) sense of *time* and *space* would be created onscreen. Put another way, although each shot had been filmed separately in completely different locations, editing would create the impression of a single place and time.

In general, Hollywood films attempt to mask editing within scenes—to make the action appear to be seamless by matching shots in ways that make the cuts seem invisible. Shots are matched in three key ways: by action, by graphic content, and by the direction in which characters are looking. *Matching on action* involves the use of motion to create a visual bridge between shots. For instance, shot A is a shot of a pole vaulter going over the bar from left to right and beginning to fall out of the image, and shot B is a shot of the vaulter falling into the image and hitting the padding. *Graphic matches* are made according to the shapes and positions of the objects being filmed. For example, characters in conversation with each other tend to remain in the same positions onscreen. If character A is on the right side of the screen and character B is on the left, graphic matches ensure that they will remain so in subsequent shots. (Consider the opposite: if the characters *did not* maintain the same graphic position in the image, they would appear to flip back and forth.) Finally, *eye-line matches* maintain continuity between shots by way of the direction of characters' lines of vision. Shot A contains a woman on the left of the image; she is looking down at something she is reading, but then suddenly looks up, offscreen, to the left. Shot B contains another woman, also on the left of the image. For the woman in shot B to appear to see the woman in shot A, in which direction must she look? (Note that these shots are not matched graphically; both characters are on the left of the image. Instead, the shots are matched on the basis of the direction the characters are looking.) The correct answer is that the woman in shot B looks to the right of the image.

If shots are like building blocks, editing within individual scenes creates a series of modular units which, in turn, must be pieced together. Editing from scene to scene accomplishes this task. In this type of editing, there are five basic transitions: the cut, the fade-in or fade-out, the dissolve, the iris, and the wipe. Cutting between scenes occurs by the same means as cutting within scenes: one piece of film is spliced onto another. Here, however, classical Hollywood does not attempt to mask the cut with matching devices because the goal is to keep the scenes spatially and/or temporally distinct in the audience's mind. In a process called *crosscutting* or *parallel action*, two scenes occurring simultaneously but in two different places are edited together. Such juxtaposition of scenes can be used to heighten suspense, as in the following example. Scene A contains shots of a car racing down a highway, together with shots of the man driving the car, while scene B contains shots of a pregnant woman walking into a hospital. Given the proper setup in terms of the characters' identities, crosscutting between these two scenes may suggest that the man in the car is attempting to reach the hospital to be with his wife when she gives birth.

Fading in, *fading out*, and *dissolving* provide a way of smoothing transitions between scenes. In a fade-in, the image begins either in complete darkness or whiteness and gradually takes form on the screen; in a fade-out, of course, the opposite occurs. In a *dissolve*, one shot fades in as another fades out, creating a superimposition effect in the middle. In the silent era, a common transition was the *iris-out*, in which the image begins as a kind of peephole which then expands outward. An *iris-in* achieves the opposite effect. Finally, *wipes* produce a sort of windshield-wiper effect on the screen, as one image appears to push the other off the screen from side to side, from the middle, in the shape of an expanding circle or star, and so on. Wipes were common in films of the 1920s and 1930s; they have become popular again in music videos.

These are the basic terms you will need to describe what you see on the screen. Your textbook probes their meaning further by combining formal analysis with discussions of Hollywood history, narrative structure, and genre. As you proceed through the course, try not only to notice the formal elements of the clips featured in the programs but also to describe these elements in your mind as they occur onscreen.

Thinking and Writing About Film

INTRODUCTION

This course is designed to help you see films more critically—to look beneath the surface of the movies by learning to appreciate just how complex that simple-looking surface may be. While you are learning about Hollywood's history and economics, its cultural importance and the meaning of various genres, you are also learning about some of the cinema's formal aspects. In a way, learning to analyze film art from a formal perspective is the most difficult aspect of the course, because although you may understand the technical terms used to describe film style, you may not be able to use this language yourself without some practice.

Since your experience with film criticism has probably been limited to movie reviews in newspapers and magazines, and since this course tends not to deal with films in that way, you may find yourself wondering what kind of writing is expected of you here. This supplementary unit provides an introduction to critical writing about films by offering a sample student analysis of the film *Scarlet Street*, a 1945 film noir directed by Fritz Lang. Throughout the analysis you will see footnotes. These notes are not references to the sources of quotations or paraphrasings, but rather a running commentary on the analysis itself—an explanation of its structure and mechanics. Some of these notes have particular application to film papers; others pertain to any kind of critical writing you are asked to do in your college career.

Writing about film resembles other types of critical writing—analyses of novels, poetry, or paintings, for instance—in that its goal is to bring the underlying meanings of a given work of art into the open and explain these meanings in as clear, as detailed, and as convincing a way as possible. The object is not to summarize the film in capsule form, nor is it to present a collection of other critics' opinions, though each of these activities may play a limited role in your work. (Because you may or may not have access to other critical writing on the films you choose to write about in this course, the sample analysis offered here contains no quotations or paraphrasings from published critical material on *Scarlet Street*. Such material may add to your understanding of a film, but it is not necessary to write a close analysis.) Instead, the object of the paper is to encounter a film directly and to fashion a coherent argument about its meaning.

To prepare for writing such an analysis, see the whole film at least once. Select a sequence that seems to you to be particularly interesting and important, and examine that sequence as closely as possible. If you have access to a VCR or DVD player, you will have the opportunity to go through the scene repeatedly and take detailed notes, stopping and starting at will. If you have no such access, your job will be more difficult, but it can still be done by being as observant as possible while the sequence is running and by taking notes as quickly and efficiently as you can.

Because this sample paper is relatively short (most college courses assign papers in the range of 5 to 7 pages), the analysis centers on only one sequence from *Scarlet Street*. It is impossible to write a detailed analysis of an entire film in a paper of average length. The end result would be necessarily incomplete and full of broad generalizations. Instead, this student's paper attempts to construct a more manageable argument by analyzing one scene in detail. The introductory and concluding paragraphs suggest that the sequence in question is important to the larger theme and design of the film, but by limiting the paper's scope, the specific points it makes become all the more provable, and the argument therefore becomes all the more convincing.

By no means must you have seen *Scarlet Street* in order to use this sample paper. Simply by following the tenor of the argument and the structure of the essay, you will learn how to construct a close analysis of any film you choose.

Finally, this paper is not the final word on *Scarlet Street*, nor is it the only possible reading of the sequence in question. In your own papers, do not feel that you have to provide a comprehensive reading of a film. Instead, try to build the best, most carefully reasoned argument you can. And, of course, feel free to take issue with the conclusions drawn here.

MIRROR, MIRROR: THE MURDER SEQUENCE IN *SCARLET STREET*

A film about female deceit and male violence, Fritz Lang's *Scarlet Street* presents a world of sexual tension in which resolution occurs only through murder and insanity. Oppressive, anxious, and claustrophobic, Lang's vision of male-female relations casts women as selfish shrews and men as either abusive, hypermasculine creeps or emasculated dupes.[1] In both cases, these representations are split, each in their own way. The two types of men are embodied by two different characters, while the image of women is contained in one character who is seen in two different ways. These split images come together in a moment of profound violence—the murder sequence, when the meek male's sudden psychological breakdown leads him to kill the deceitful woman, a crisis Lang expresses through reflected images, misinterpreted sounds, and contrasting colors.[2]

The protagonist of the film, a mild-mannered clerk named Christopher Cross, begins as the second type of male—small, gentlemanly, and foolish.

But when he discovers that Kitty, the woman he loves, has betrayed him for the former type, represented by a drunken, violent con artist named Johnny, he resolves his psychological crisis in a spurt of rage, stabbing her to death with an ice pick as she lies in bed.[3] By murdering Kitty, Chris reveals that beneath his gentle facade lurks a more primal, Johnny-like nature. As his very name suggests, Chris Cross has been at war with himself all along.

The murder sequence begins with a medium long shot of Kitty, lying in bed and talking on the telephone. The bed and the area surrounding it are bright white in color; the bed has an elaborate, tufted white bedboard, and the sheets and comforter are white as well. Kitty is wearing a form-fitting satin negligee, which is also white and somewhat reflective. And a mirror beside the bed further reflects this dazzling array of white material. This suggestive mise-en-scene calls to mind Kitty's introduction in the film in the scene in which Chris rushes to her aid on a Greenwich Village street as she is being beaten by Johnny. At that point, Kitty is wearing a transparent raincoat, a suggestive touch of costuming that implies that she is a woman who can (or should be) seen through.[4] Here, the whiteness of the mise-en-scene is another ironic comment on Kitty's character. On the one hand, she has deceived Chris into viewing her as a virginal, uncorrupt, virtuous woman, as white as fresh snow. On the other hand, the amount of white in her bedroom is excessive and overdone, suggesting that her virtue is an all-too-obvious act—obvious, that is, to the viewer, if not yet to Chris.

In the first of two important confusions of sound in the sequence, a sudden noise is heard on the sound track—a noise which Kitty misinterprets as the sound of Johnny returning to her apartment. In fact, it is Chris who has returned. To express this confusion, Lang cuts from the medium long shot of Kitty on the bed to a long shot of the door beginning to open, then back to Kitty lying back on the bed and saying "Come on, Johnny, I heard you," and finally back to the door opening and Chris coming in, dressed in a black overcoat and carrying a black hat.

Chris's costume provides an important contrast to Kitty's all-white bedroom, and because he is slightly hunched over as he enters, his presence seems all the more malevolent even though he is still in the role of the meek and pathetic suitor. But this is not the only contrast Lang reveals in this sequence. As Kitty leans back in the bed, her face is reflected in the mirror, thus splitting her image in two. Throughout the sequence, Kitty's face appears, disappears, and reappears in this mirror, suggesting that her double identity—Chris's image of her as virtuous contrasted with her real nature as a deceiver—is reaching a moment of crisis.[5]

When Chris approaches the bed, the camera pans left with him. When he reaches the bed, the shot becomes a two-shot, with each character at the edge of the image—Kitty, in white on the left, and Chris in black on the right.[6] Their contrasting positions, as well as the colors of their costumes, suggests the great emotional distance between them, a gap which is further expressed by Chris's dialogue and Kitty's subsequent reaction. "You lied to me, Kitty,"

Chris says with a tone not of rage but of foolish disappointment. "Can I help it if I'm in love?" she casually responds. As she says this line, Kitty leans back seductively in bed, a physical gesture which not only expresses her lack of interest in Chris but also causes her face to reappear in the mirror. By directing the actress to move in such a way as to appear twice in the same image, Lang reveals the two aspects of Kitty at the same time—Chris's pristine vision of her versus her deceptive reality.

Despite Kitty's offhand, bored treatment of Chris, he cannot face the truth of his relationship with her. With both characters still seen in two shot on opposite sides of the image, Chris declares that he is no longer married, that he is "free"—an ironic comment, given that he has never been more trapped in a bad relationship than he is at this moment. Kitty turns quickly away from him and throws herself face down on the bed—another effort to hide her true self from him.[7]

At this point, another ambiguous noise is heard on the soundtrack. Muffled and indistinct, the sound is understood in two different ways; like Kitty's image, the noise is itself split. The audience, having seen Kitty from a clearer perspective than Chris's, knows the truth about Kitty's deceit and therefore hears the sound as laughter. Chris, on the other hand, is still captivated by his false image of her and thus misunderstands the sound as crying. Underscoring the ambiguity of the sound is the fact that at this moment there is no image of Kitty's face on the screen at all—neither in the bed nor in the mirror.

Lang then cuts to a medium shot of Chris, looking toward the left of the image. He reaches with his hand to the left, and Lang pans and tracks slightly to reveal Kitty's body as Chris touches her back. "Don't cry, Kitty. Please don't cry," he says.

The laughing/crying noise is louder now, and as it gets even louder, it becomes increasingly distinct as laughter. Suddenly, Kitty turns around in bed and sits up. Not only does her face become visible in the mirror at this point, but the face in the mirror is much more distinct and visible than the real one because Kitty has turned away from the camera, causing the mirror's image to appear clearly to the audience in 3/4 angle. Both images direct their gaze in the direction of Chris, who is thus presented with a clear double-vision of the woman with whom he has fallen in love. "I'm not crying, you fool," she snaps. "I'm laughing!"

Lang cuts to a slightly low angle medium shot of Chris, who takes a step backward as if reeling from a blow, then cuts back to a slightly high angle of Kitty as she declares, "Oh, you idiot! How could a man be so dumb?" Cutting back to Chris, who takes another step back, Lang then pans a bit to the right as Chris knocks an ice pick off the counter. The camera tilts down and then back up as Chris leans over and picks it up, all to the tune of the laughing sound, which is continuous and distinct.[8]

By cutting back and forth between Kitty and Chris several more times, Lang separates the two characters spatially as well as emotionally. These two characters will be seen in the same image together only once more, and the union will prove to be fatal for one of them. For now, though, Lang maintains and develops the growing tension by keeping them apart. Having finally revealed the side of herself that she has kept suppressed in an effort to deceive Chris, Kitty lets it all come out with a vengeance. "I've wanted to laugh in your face ever since I first met you!" she barks. "You're old and ugly and I'm sick of you! Sick! Sick! Sick!"

Lang cuts to a medium shot of Chris clutching the ice pick and saying, "Kitty, for heaven's sake!" He then cuts back to Kitty, who defiantly puts her hands on her hips and cruelly contrasts Chris to Johnny by saying *"He's a man!"* She orders Chris to leave, pointing to the door, but her expression quickly changes from domination to fear. The camera does not move as Kitty jumps back in the bed and screams "Get away from me! Chris! Chris!"

Lang cuts to a medium shot of Chris advancing with the ice pick, then back to Kitty, who dives into her all-white bed in a futile effort to shield herself from him. He enters the image on the right, his black outfit suddenly contrasting with the whiteness of the sheets, and he begins to stab her through the covers. The actual stabbing is very quick, especially given the fact that this is the culmination of their relationship. After only a few seconds, Lang cuts away from this act of violence to the exterior of the building, where Johnny is about to crash his car into a fire hydrant.

Kitty's white bed, the figurative object not only of Chris's desire but also of his suppressed rage, ultimately envelopes Kitty as she attempts to hide herself from him for the last time, yet Chris finally achieves a kind of mastery over both the bed and the woman in it through the act of murder. By cutting through the bedcovers, Chris finally pierces Kitty's false facade. Although this is not the only time in the sequence in which the two characters are seen in the same shot together, their final encounter brings them physically together in a moment of violence which is almost explicitly sexual, given that this is the first and only time Kitty has been in bed with Chris. From Chris's perspective, Kitty's murder could not take place in a more appropriate setting.[9]

But as his paintings demonstrate, Chris has no perspective. The murder is an irrational act, but it is only one of many involving Chris's feelings toward Kitty. Like the rest of his relationship with Kitty, Chris's attempt to resolve his rage is deluded, for he will never escape its consequences. Lang films the actual killing so quickly, cutting away from the stabbing almost immediately, that there is no emotional payoff, no perverse satisfaction. The tension revolving around Chris's feelings toward Kitty therefore does not end here, but instead continues on throughout the rest of the film in the form of guilt—the increasingly oppressive, claustrophobic feeling Chris bears.

In one of the final sequences of the film, Chris is alone in a dark, seedy hotel room, immersed in the shadowy world of his guilt.[10] Plagued by Kitty's disembodied voice taunting him, Chris is forced to repeat the nightmarish sound confusion begun in the murder sequence. In Kitty's bedroom, the site of his deepest suppressed wishes, Chris's failure to hear a sound correctly led to an explosion of rage. Here, in the hotel room, the sounds have taken on a life of their own, and he is equally unable to distinguish between his imagination and reality. The fragmentation to which Lang subjects Kitty's image by way of the bedroom mirror is repeated here in sound form as Kitty's voice is reflected through memory and guilt. *Scarlet Street*'s vision of women may be cruelly misogynistic, but the unsatisfactory resolutions Lang offers to men—violence and insanity—are almost as desperate and certainly as inescapable.[11]

NOTES

[1]Begin by assuming that your reader (your professor, most likely) is familiar with the film you are discussing. Sometimes, students become overwhelmed by feeling that they must describe the whole film before getting down to the specific topic at hand, just in case the reader doesn't know much about it. Here, the student begins the paper by presenting a general introduction to the theme of the film but assumes that the reader has some familiarity with the subject. Later, for the sake of clarity, the central characters will be introduced, but only in specific, descriptive terms that further develop the argument of the paper.

[2]This sentence functions as the thesis statement of the paper—the single sentence which presents in capsule form the argument made throughout the rest of the paper. From this sentence, the reader knows (a) that the murder sequence is going to be analyzed in detail and (b) that the student thinks that the sequence is formally concerned with the film's central conflict. Allowing for periodic digressions which add substance to the argument, the rest of the paper will be a point-by-point attempt to prove the truth of what the student has claimed.

[3]This paragraph further clarifies the thesis statement contained at the end of the first paragraph by naming the three central characters and describing in more specific terms the sequence in question.

[4]Although this detail refers to an earlier scene, it is appropriate to mention here for several reasons. First, it adds a revealing detail about Kitty's character. Second, it demonstrates that Lang's mise-en-scene is expressive throughout the film. Third, by referring to an important earlier scene, the student suggests that his command of the material goes beyond the small sequence being analyzed, thereby (hopefully) convincing the reader that he knows what he is talking about.

[5]In this paragraph the student is attempting to describe not only the details seen on the screen but also the meanings those details generate—in other words, to interpret the sequence. While the descriptive details are factual, the meanings ascribed to them are not. Therefore, to be convincing, the student needs to tie these meanings as closely as possible to the factual formal details of the sequence. The student may be wrong in his interpretations, but he has attempted to ground his opinions in fact.

[6]Keep grounding your observations in factual details about the film, and describe these details using the terms you have learned in Supplementary Unit A: "Film Language." For the precise definition of terms, refer back to that chapter, to your textbook, and to the glossary at the end of this Study Guide.

[7]This paragraph, and all subsequent ones until the concluding paragraph, attempt to build the argument by accumulating concrete details and interpretations. The effect is to say to the reader, "I am proving that what I have said is correct by citing this, and this, and this, and this. . . ." At the same time, each paragraph raises a slightly different point; repeating the *same* point from paragraph to paragraph will convince the reader that you have seen only one aspect of the film.

[8]Not every paragraph needs to contain interpretations. Here, the student furthers the argument simply by citing concrete details about the image and sound track. One of the tasks of a formal analysis is to describe the sequence accurately—to select its most important details.

[9]The student is attempting here to bring the argument to a conclusion by offering some broad interpretations of the sequence. By this point in the paper, the student has presumably cited all the crucial details about the sequence's structure and mise-en-scene and is free to use those details to support his claims about the sequence's meaning.

[10]Having described the sequence as fully as he is able, the student concludes the paper by tying it in with another important sequence that occurs later in the film. Instead of simply providing a summary of points that have already been raised in the paper (a strategy which risks boring the reader by merely repeating what he or she has already read), the student attempts to convince the reader that he has understood not only the individual sequence but also the film as a whole.

[11]With this final sentence, the student refers back to the first paragraph of the paper and the thesis sentence contained there. In part, this is a restatement of the thesis and the argument it makes about the film's theme, but the student's hope is that the reader will have come to a new understanding of the theme by way of the points raised throughout the paper.

Classical Hollywood Style Today

I. INTRODUCTION

In what form do the techniques and devices of classical Hollywood cinema survive today? Are contemporary mainstream films still considered to be classical? How do they differ from films of the past? How is classical style "read" by contemporary audiences? Are there options for diversity in classical style, or is it essentially a white-, heterosexual-, and male-dominated cinema?

By addressing questions like this, this unit serves both to summarize the course and the issues contained in it and to introduce in capsule form some further issues of theory and practice. In the telecourse program, you will see several practicing filmmakers and critics discuss the state of relatively contemporary Hollywood filmmaking. To broaden this discussion to include still other voices and perspectives, this Study Guide unit is composed of brief excerpts of interviews and critical writing—commentary from informed directors, critics, and scholars on a variety of topics revolving around classical style. The sources of these quotes are cited in footnotes. Use any or all of these quotations as the basis for further thought and research.

Note the fact that there can be productive disagreement about the nature of Hollywood's art and industry. The American cinema is an institution, but like the wider culture out of which it has grown, it is still evolving. Shifting audience expectations, changing views about gender and race, fluctuating economic trends, developing and declining genres—these variables continue to inform and change the nature of Hollywood films. But remember: our understanding of these changes is not scientific. Film historians use concrete details to ground their arguments about the meaning of films and the culture that produces them, but in general their conclusions are arguable. There is not total agreement among the experts quoted below, and that's a good thing. The goal of this unit is not only to provide you with information, but also to spark debate.

CLASSICAL STYLE AND "THE NEW HOLLYWOOD"

Film historians David Bordwell and Janet Staiger argue that despite their technological inventiveness, their emulation of foreign art cinema directors, and the influence of film schools and formal film culture on their work, filmmakers such as Martin Scorsese, Francis Coppola, Brian De Palma, and other so-called New Hollywood directors have not significantly revised American film practice. In fact, they argue, the work of these directors tends to be conservative and genre-bound:

"No recent American director has produced an idiosyncratic style comparable to even Truffaut's or Bergman's, let alone to that of Antonioni or Bresson. The classical premises of time and space remain powerfully in force, with only minor instrumental changes (e.g., multiple cameras to capture reverse angles, zooms doing duty for tracking shots). Altman, probably the most interesting stylist to emerge in the New Hollywood, nonetheless uses techniques in ways which conform to the dominant paradigm. . . .Even the most ambitious directors cannot escape genres. New Hollywood cinema consists of gangster and outlaw films, thrillers, Westerns, musicals, science-fiction films, comedies, and an occasional melodrama. *Apocalypse Now* is primarily and almost entirely a war movie. *Blue Collar*, a film of putative social significance, includes fight scenes reminiscent of prison films like *Brute Force* (1947), a caper intrigue, and even a car chase. Classical film style and codified genres swallow up art-film borrowings, taming the (already limited) disruptiveness of the art cinema."[1]

NEW TECHNOLOGIES

Throughout Hollywood history, new technologies not only have broadened the range of expressive techniques open to filmmakers but also have expanded the very definition of cinema. At the same time, skepticism about technology on the part of critics and theorists has been rampant. Innovations that later proved to be of vital importance to the medium have been attacked as extraneous, corrupting influences on the art form; sound film, widescreen processes, and color were each derided as gimmicks when they were introduced. On the other hand, certain filmmakers have been eager to embrace new technologies and the profound changes they may bring. Here is Francis Coppola on the subject of current and future technologies:

"The climate of our times is very tired. It's not that we have fewer ideas so much as something in the culture that doesn't allow itself new approaches. Technology is delivering new values that have yet to be tapped. We've got all this new stuff and people aren't looking at the obvious, which is that something totally new in terms of stories can come about. Instead, we use the advances in technology to reproduce and reiterate what we've already seen, what's been done in terms of form for centuries. I think it's time we catch up with the tools that have been invented.

What I'm saying is that technology, if used in new ways, might break up the monopoly certain imagery, certain icons, have on our attention. I think we could see a less homogenized view of things, and we'll have to if there's going to be a shake-up in our current political thinking. There's something in our politics as old, as dated, as those stories from ancient times that get endlessly recycled."[2]

HOLLYWOOD AND RACE

In very recent years, several African-American directors have risen to prominence in Hollywood. Spike Lee (*Do the Right Thing, Malcolm X*), Robert Townsend (*Hollywood Shuffle*), and John Singleton (*Boyz N the Hood*) have begun to break down the American film industry's racial barrier by making mainstream films about African-Americans. However, Hollywood continues to distinguish between audiences on the basis of race. As Spike Lee has noted, film industry executives tend to see American audiences as African-Americans on the one hand and everybody else on the other:

"Hollywood still believes that whites won't go to a black film. Everybody runs from the word 'black.' To Hollywood, black is death at the box-office. [But] there is a desperate need in the marketplace for black product. Black people are dying to see themselves portrayed realistically. Nobody is doing that type of film. . . . [*School Daze*] was scheduled to open the same day as *Action Jackson* and *Shoot to Kill*. They wanted me to change [the release date]. They were worried that there would be too many black films out there. Too many people here think of blacks as a monolithic group."[3]

HOLLYWOOD AND GENDER

Feminist critics have attacked Hollywood filmmaking on various grounds. Some criticize the relatively frequent cruelty to which female characters are subjected; others attack the scarcity of women hired as directors. One of the most radical critiques has been leveled by Laura Mulvey, a British film theorist who sees the very mechanisms of classical Hollywood style to be male dominated—the camera's gaze as a means of male oppression. Mulvey's argument is too detailed to summarize fairly here, but the following fragment sketches her position in regard to Hollywood films and gender:

"It is helpful to understand what the cinema has been, how its magic has worked in the past, while attempting a theory and a practice which will challenge this cinema of the past. Psychoanalytic theory is thus appropriated here as a political weapon, demonstrating the way the unconscious of patriarchal society has structured film form. . . . The magic of the Hollywood style at its best (and of all the cinema which fell within its sphere of influence) arose, not exclusively, but in one important aspect, from its skilled and satisfying manipulation of visual pleasure. Unchallenged, mainstream film coded the erotic into the language of the dominant patriarchal order. . . . Women, whose image has continually been stolen and used for this end, cannot view the decline of the traditional film form with anything much more than sentimental regret."[4]

HOLLYWOOD AND SEXUAL ORIENTATION

Feminist critics are not alone in finding Hollywood cinema to be oppressive in terms of gender and sexuality. Gay critics have become increasingly vocal about Hollywood's depiction of gay men and lesbians. Like African-Americans, gay men and lesbians have looked to the screen hoping to see accurate representations of their lives and instead found distortions; where African-Americans tend to see a steady stream of comical servants and nameless muggers, gay men and lesbians see a procession of wimps, psychotics, and suicides—caricatures regularly described in the standard vocabulary of anti-gay language. Critic Vito Russo comments on images of gay men and lesbians in Hollywood films:

"When for the first time two men kissed onscreen [in Sidney Lumet's *A View from the Bridge*, one of the characters'] accusatory *'That's* what you are!' burned a hole in the consciousness of an invisible gay audience. The movies, gays thought, had spoken their name. For it is not gay actors or gay characters but the *idea* of homosexuality for which gays have searched in films, almost always in vain. But the decision to make visible the gay lifestyle is irrevocable, and eventually the movies will have to reflect the diversity of gay experience.

Invisibility is the great enemy. It has prevented the truth from being heard, and it will continue to do so as long as the celluloid closet is inhabited by lesbians and gay men who serve Hollywood's idea of homosexuality. In 1975, a group of producers and directors, some of them reputedly closet gays, walked out of a screening of Robert Aldrich's *The Choirboys*, reportedly because of its anti-gay language. 'Those guys who walked out are some of our most successful directors,' Aldrich says, 'and if they're walking out but not talking in public about why they walked out, then they're not the ones who are going to make the breakthrough films about homosexuals. They're going to stay in the mainstream and direct action pictures. It's the old joke: I'm on board, pull up the ladder.'

There never have been lesbians or gay men in Hollywood films. Only homosexuals."[5]

THE INDUSTRY: PAST AND PRESENT

Thomas Schatz, a film scholar who has traced the rise and fall of the studio system, explains that although Hollywood created some of great cultural landmarks, the mechanisms for making films of this sort no longer exist. For Schatz, what classical Hollywood did best cannot be done again:

"At the heart of the classical Hollywood and of each studio's house style were those star-genre formulations, the Davis melodramas and Karloff horror pictures and Gene Kelly musicals that seemed to flow so effortlessly from the filmmaking machinery. Those were the economic lifeblood of the studio system and the basis for the industry's popular appeal, and they still stand among the greatest cultural accomplishments in an age when art and industry, commerce and technology are so inexorably wed. As Hollywood classics like *Jezebel* and *Frankenstein* and *On the Town* are recirculated and rediscovered by successive generations, it is little wonder that filmmakers would want to revive the system that produced them. But those celluloid traces, at once so real and so remote, are all that remain of the studio system and of the vigorous, dynamic breed that created and sustained it."[6]

In the past, directors were rarely able to get their names "above the title" in credits. Now, directors appear to have more clout, at least in terms of contractual details such as crediting themselves; it is not uncommon to see the phrase "A [name] Film" in the ads for even the most ordinary action-adventure film. However, this increased respect for the work of a director is not always translated into practical terms. Directors who want to make personal films find it to be at least as difficult now as it was in the days of the studio system. For a director like Martin Scorsese, the old Hollywood continues to have its own mystique:

"The industry is now run by businessmen and if I want to continue to make personal films, I have to show them I have some sort of respect for money, and that it will actually show on the screen. People talk about the great old days of the movie moguls, but that was a different time. I think all the great studio filmmakers are dead or no longer working. I don't put myself, my friends, and other contemporary filmmakers in their category. I just see us doing some work. The studios were over by when I began in the early seventies: the old system was a whole different period, a closed, naive world truthful unto itself. Everything now is too open, too international. I once met Andre De Toth in California, and he said to me, 'Harry Cohn was a difficult man, but we made pictures then, young man, we made pictures!' And he was right."[7]

NOTES

[1]David Bordwell and Janet Staiger. "Historical Implications of the Classical Hollywood Cinema," in David Bordwell, Janet Staiger, and Kristin Thompson, *The Classical Hollywood Cinema*. New York: Columbia University Press, 1985, p. 375.

[2]Ric Gentry. "Interview with Francis Coppola," *Post Script 6*, no. 3 (Spring/Summer 1987): 2-3.

[3]Betsy Sharkey. "Knocking on Hollywood's Door," *American Film* (July/August 1989): 24-25.

[4]Laura Mulvey. "Visual Pleasure and Narrative Cinema," *Screen 16*, no. 3 (Autumn, 1975). Reprinted in Bill Nichols, ed., *Movies and Methods*, Vol. 2. Berkeley: University of California Press, 1985.

[5]Vito Russo. *The Celluloid Closet*. New York: Harper & Row, 1987, pp. 244-245.

[6]Thomas Schatz. *The Genius of the System*. New York: Pantheon Books, 1988, p. 492.

[7]Martin Scorsese. *Scorsese on Scorsese*. Edited by David Thompson and Ian Christie. Boston: Faber & Faber, 1989, p. 114.

Answers and Examples

UNIT 1

1. This exercise is designed not only to show you how much you know (or think you know) about Hollywood, but also to gauge your commitment to this course. If you came up with a list of only three or four obvious words, you have not put much thought into it. Ask yourself what you are trying to get out of your education. If your list is longer and more varied in its content, save it; by comparing it to the work you are producing at the end of the course you will have a good idea of how much you have learned.

2. If you had difficulty finding such an interview or article, and you did not ask a librarian for help, you will need to learn some essential research methods before proceeding in this course. Don't be shy; ask for help. Your instructor will be able to give you general guidance, and a librarian will show you how to find any books and periodicals you need.

3. Here is a sequence using three shots; *this is only an example*. There is no right answer; the sequence could take any number of forms. *(a)* The camera is placed on the middle row of seats on one side of the court so that most of the opposite side of the stadium is visible in long shot, along with most of the court; the crowd is cheering wildly. *(b)* The same angle, but much closer. People are seen cheering and clapping; if you look closely, you can see that one fan is not cheering. *(c)* Still closer. Six fans are visible, but only five of them are cheering. One person is sitting perfectly still, staring straight ahead. The camera tracks toward the sullen person, continuing until the person's dark, staring eyes fill the frame.

4. Supplementary Unit B in the Study Guide contains a sample close analysis, treating both formal and thematic issues. Use it as a general guide throughout this course. For this simpler initial exercise, however, judge your work more leniently. See how many descriptive details you have noted in each shot. Are your descriptions clear? Were you able to see how the different shots related to each other on a formal level? Were you able to draw any conclusions about the *meaningful* relationships

between shots? This is a fairly difficult initial assignment; by the end of the course you will be able to understand these relationships more clearly.

ANSWERS TO SELF TEST

1. (a) Mise-en-scene consists of all of the different meaningful elements within the shot (including lighting, set design, costume), together with the formal elements of the shot itself (camera angle, camera distance, composition, and so on).

   (b) Segmentation is a structural analysis of a film's narrative, dividing it into its basic units.

   (c) *Citizen Kane* was Orson Welles's first film, which has had a profound influence on the American cinema.

   (d) Joseph Mankiewicz directed *All About Eve* and other films.

   (e) Three-point lighting is the standard lighting setup in Hollywood films, designed to suggest three sources of light—the key light, the fill light, and the back light.

   (f) Dramatic unities is a term in classical drama, that refers to the unity of action, time, and/or space.

   (g) Modernism is a term that describes 20th-century art which conveys the era's spirit of crisis by rejecting the principles of order, regularity, and invisibility that characterized earlier artistic periods.

   (h) Seamless editing is the technique of making transitions between shots as unnoticeable as possible.

2. (a) is false.

3. The technique known as "matching" conceals potential discontinuities between shots when they are edited together. There are three main types of matches: eye-line matches, which match according to the direction a character is looking onscreen; matching on action, in which movements begun in one shot are carried through in the next shot; and graphic matches, which bridge cuts by matching the compositional elements of each shot.

4. (a) true; (b) false; (c) false; (d) true.

5. Classical Hollywood style is a formal and narrative style of filmmaking centering on individual characters in pursuit of their goals. In general, the style seeks to maintain narrative continuity by focusing on an individual, with most if not all of the film's events either leading toward or preventing the character from reaching his or her goal. Formally, the classical style tries to achieve semitransparency by putting itself almost completely at the service of the narrative, with elements of mise-en-

scene and editing working to advance the narrative and develop characters. Stylistic invisibility thus becomes one of the main goals of classical style. Through such techniques as seamless editing and expressive camera movements, lighting, costume design, and other formal elements, classical Hollywood style seeks to remain unnoticed. However, these techniques not only express the narrative; they *are* the narrative. As such, the self-effacing methods that characterize classical Hollywood style can never really disappear from view.

UNIT 2

1. One quick, simple way of grading this exercise is to show it to someone else and ask him or her if the diagram makes any sense. If you cannot do this, ask yourself if the branches are clearly drawn and connected. See if they are clear *intellectually* as well as visually!

2. It's your film, and since the choices are all yours, there can be no right or wrong answers. One way of judging your work is to go back to the textbook and see how many departments you included in your production and how many you forgot. In addition, grade yourself on the level of specificity you achieved. Did you flesh out your tale with significant concrete details? As a sample story, here is the beginning of a reasonably detailed, admittedly satirical tale of the studio system:

   While flipping through the current issue of *Modern Anxiety* magazine, a reader in the story department comes upon a short story she thinks would make a good movie—"I, Voodoo Priest." She writes a memo to the producer, who quickly buys the rights to the story without having read it and assigns a studio screenwriter to write the screenplay. While the script is being written, the producer casts two actors under long-term contract to the studio—Dolores Blythe, who is known for being a sultry, "dangerous woman" type, and Tommy Dallas, a popular cowboy star whose films usually make money. After reading the finished script and expressing his unqualified approval, the producer gives it to a second screenwriter and tells her to shift the film away from the Caribbean island on which it had been set and rewrite it so that it takes place in a Nevada rodeo. The title is changed, too; now it's called *Wrangler*. A director, also under contract, is assigned; he has already made 20 inexpensive Westerns for the studio, so the head of the studio trusts him to bring it in on budget. . . .

3. Only you can gauge the accuracy of your own biographical research. In terms of detail, you may have simply paraphrased a short biographical entry in a film dictionary. A much better job would have been to take

the time to find and read a more extensive biography or two, either in book-length form or in a comprehensive film encyclopedia. Have you answered the question of why your director moved from studio to studio (if in fact he did move)? Did he fight with the studio bosses? Did he get better offers from rivals? And do critics find that his style changed in any appreciable way, or was he able to retain his individuality—or both? Have you cited your sources for this information?

4. Writing in support of studio authorship, you might have cited the studios' use of exclusive long-term contracts and the consequent reappearance of stars and other creative talents over a matter of years. You could argue that 20th Century-Fox's repeated use of Shirley Temple, for example, helps to define at least one aspect of Fox's corporate world view. You might note the ability of a studio boss such as M-G-M's L. B. Mayer to impose his taste on several decades of filmmaking at his studio. Or, you could argue from a theoretical stance, seeing ownership as a sort of authorship. To deny the idea of studio authorship, you might cite the complexity of the studio's corporate structure as precluding *any* authorial voice at all. Or, you might argue that directors or screenwriters are the real authors of films. Or, you might take a conciliatory position, seeing films as having multiple authors, in which case you might have attempted to explain how each signature comes to be understood by the audience. In any case, this is a difficult question, one that many critics have failed to answer. Give yourself some points just for trying.

ANSWERS TO SELF TEST

1. *(a)* An oligopoly is the exclusive or near-exclusive ownership of a given industry by several companies acting in concert.
   (b) Vertical integration is the studios' control not only of the production of films but also their distribution and exhibition.
   (c) The story department consists of a staff of professional readers employed by the studio to find and develop script ideas out of newspaper and magazine articles, plays, and books.
   (d) Block booking is the tactic of forcing exhibitors to rent films in groups rather than individually. For instance, a potential hit would be linked with three potential bombs, so if theater owners wanted to show the hit, they would have to rent the bombs as well.
   (e) Radio-Keith-Orpheum (RKO) was one of the five major studios in Hollywood during the studio era.
   (f) *United States v. Paramount Pictures, Inc. et al.* is the Supreme Court decision which ruled that the studio system constituted an oligopoly

because it depended on such illegal practices as blind bidding and block booking.

(g) Blind bidding is a standard practice during the studio era in which an exhibitor was forced to rent a film from a studio without ever having been given the chance to see it or learn anything about it.

(h) "Minors" was the name given to the three smaller studios in Hollywood during the studio era—Columbia, Universal, and United Artists.

2. (a) and (b) are false.

3. Short answer: The studio system ended after the Supreme Court ruled in the late 1940s that the studios were engaging in unfair business practices by owning not only film production facilities but also distribution and exhibition facilities, as well as forcing competing exhibitors to rent films through the practices of blind bidding and block booking. The studios were forced to divest themselves of their theater chains, thus dismantling the economic basis of the studio system.

4. (a) false; (b) true; (c) true; (d) true.

5. If you believe that the studio system hindered American film art, you could point to the regimentation of the studio system, the difficulties it presented to filmmakers who were not "team players," the factorylike manufacturing of products and the consequent suppression of individuality, and the demands of the mass marketplace as evidence. If you think that the system actually helped American film art, you might cite the large number of films produced; the system's ability to finance, produce, and market films efficiently; the number of filmmakers who seemed to work well under the system; and the popularity and longevity of individual studio-era films. In either event, judge your answer on the variety of supporting evidence you cite and the detail with which you present your case. Have you referred to specific points raised by the program's experts or by the textbook? Have you quoted anyone, even if indirectly? If so, have you cited that person properly?

UNIT 3

1. A thorough research project should result in a visual essay in the form of a scrapbook, including written commentary as well as pictures. The number of pictures you choose is not as important as your ability to select significant visual evidence from a range of sources. For example, ten pictures of Tom Cruise appearing at last year's Academy Awards would not be as effective in defining his persona as a variety of pictures—the real Tom Cruise driving a race car, Cruise as a race car driver in *Days of*

Thunder, Cruise as a warrior in *The Last Samurai*, a picture of Cruise in his underwear in *Risky Business*, and an accompanying paragraph defining Cruise's persona in terms of sexuality, athleticism, and so on.

2. Judge your essay by its detail and by how well you make an argument. For instance, if your essay centers on the fact that you like Monroe but not Madonna, or vice versa, you probably could have done better. But if you have tried to *prove* your opinion with detailed descriptions of each performer, and if you made a case based on the *ideas* suggested by these descriptions, you have succeeded. For instance, you might have chosen to analyze the different conclusions suggested by the endings of "Diamonds Are a Girl's Best Friend" and "Material Girl." (In the former, the Monroe character appears to embrace the mercenary materialism of the song's lyrics; in the latter, Madonna says she's a "material girl" but ends up riding away in a plain pickup truck, suggesting just the opposite.)

3. If you have chosen a major star, there will be a wealth of information in newspapers and magazines of the period. Check your work for concrete details. How thoroughly have you described the photos and ads you cite? What do the quotations you have selected reveal? Does your thesis contain an effective argument about the star's persona? Remember: by writing a paper you are trying to *prove* something. Finally, ask yourself if your paper is *fair*. In other words, have you tried to provide a thorough, accurate portrait of the star and the period, or have you chosen only those elements that serve your purposes?

4. Judging one's own work is not easy; judging one's own theoretical work is especially difficult. If you trust a friend's judgment, ask him or her to critique your work for its logic and clarity. If not, try gaining a fresh perspective by putting it aside for a few days before taking another look at it. Does your essay have a strong thesis? Are you making an effective argument? (Even if you are summarizing a critic's work, your own paper should state the critic's position forcefully.) Have you answered the questions you (or the critics) propose? Go through your essay paragraph by paragraph and underline or highlight each new point. How much information did you ultimately present?

ANSWERS TO SELF TEST

1. (a) Theda Bara was a silent film star born in Cincinnati but promoted as an exotic beauty from the Sahara.
   (b) The Russian theater director Konstantin Stanislavsky developed the theory of acting that came to be known as the Method.

(c) *Singin' in the Rain* is a musical made in the 1950s about movie stars facing the shift from silent to sound film.

(d) Mickey Mouse is Alfred Hitchcock's example of a perfect star.

(e) *Mildred Pierce, Grand Hotel, Rain,* and *The Women* are all films starring Joan Crawford.

(f) A persona is the cultural identity of a star, constructed from an actor's roles, publicity, and biographical details.

(g) *Rebel Without a Cause, East of Eden,* and *Giant* are all films starring James Dean.

(h) Elia Kazan is a film director known for his skill with actors and his use of Method acting techniques.

2. (a) and (c) are false.

3. Technology enabled the mass reproduction of idealized images, not only in the form of motion pictures but in newspapers and magazines as well. Film technology in particular enabled audiences to imagine themselves to be physically close to stars through the use of close-ups.

4. (a) false; (b) true; (c) false; (d) true.

5. The first movie star was a famous prize fighter (Gentlemen Jim Corbett) who was signed to an exclusive motion picture contract in 1894. Other early stars included Wild West performers like Buffalo Bill and Annie Oakley. Some of the earliest stars to become famous through their appearances in films were Florence Lawrence, Mary Pickford, and Lillian Gish, whose widely distributed filmed images expressed certain cultural needs and assumptions of the era—specifically, with these women, the late-Victorian values of chastity and obedience combined with a more modern sense of self-reliance. Stars such as Douglas Fairbanks and Charles Chaplin reflected the concerns and attitudes of the newly urbanized male: for Fairbanks, the successes and frustrations of corporate life, and for Chaplin's Tramp, the frustrations of poverty combined with a willful contempt for authority.

UNIT 4

1. There are no right or wrong answers here. Judge your journal entry on its complexity and degree of detail. Did you develop your ideas with strong, vivid details, or did you make a short list of general categories and leave it at that? Did you describe your impressions concretely, drawing on real personal experiences, or did you remain vague?

2. As a way of judging your answer, you should be able to explain why the basic scenario works in terms of Western conventions, and why each of

the ends fits the traditions of classicism and revisionism. Here is an example of a basic scenario: A lone figure, a stranger, rides into the dusty town of Ropeburn. His mission remains a mystery. He seems vaguely interested in the earthy saloon keeper, Sadie, but talks to no one else. One day a posse rides into Ropeburn gunning for the town's ineffectual sheriff. The stranger shoots the entire posse and saves the sheriff's life. Unfortunately, Sadie turns out to be the sheriff's girlfriend. The morally bankrupt sheriff, who is sent into a jealous rage when Sadie tells him that she is planning to ride off with the stranger, arranges for the stranger to meet a violent end at the hands of a hired gun at the old corral on the edge of town.

An example of a classical ending: The stranger, through skill and courage, survives the shoot-out, exposes the sheriff's corruption and cowardice, and then, in a light comedy scene, ropes him and locks him up in his own jail. The grateful townspeople hire him as the new sheriff, and he makes plans to marry Sadie and turn her into an honest, upright woman.

An example of a revisionist ending: The stranger, through skill and courage, survives the shoot-out only to return to town and shoot the corrupt sheriff in the back. He leaves without bidding Sadie farewell and exits on horseback, just as mysteriously as he had arrived.

3. Ask yourself if audiences would be entertained by your sequence. Is there enough tension to sustain interest? In what way does your sequence fit within the traditions and conventions of the genre? In what ways does it add something new? Give yourself points for colorful descriptions. A brief example that uses the basic scenario and revisionist ending from Exercise 2 as a starting point follows; yours should be even more detailed. In the first shot of the shoot-out sequence, the stranger (who hasn't shaved in five days and probably hasn't bathed, either) is seen in long shot stalking behind the wall of the saloon. In the second shot, the sheriff—who looks like a young Robert Redford and is wearing freshly pressed clothes and a very shiny badge—is seen in medium close up smirking in the mirror of a barbershop. The camera tracks back as he stands up and exits the barbershop, away from the camera. For the third shot, the camera is outside the barbershop to record the sheriff coming out of the building, down a few wooden steps, and onto the dusty, empty street, all in long shot. In the fourth shot, a medium close up, the stranger reveals the shotgun he has been holding; he aims the gun and cocks it. In the fifth shot, the sheriff is seen in long shot kicking a beagle that has wandered over to greet him. The fifth shot is a close up of the sheriff's handsome, smiling face; the dog's yelp is heard on the sound track. A loud shot is then heard; the sheriff's smile freezes into a grimace as he drops out of the frame. The sixth shot is a close up of the

stranger, who has a look of satisfied disgust. He spits, and turns away. Extra Credit: Answers may vary.

4. See Supplementary Unit B: "Thinking and Writing About Film," for a sample close analysis.

ANSWERS TO SELF TEST

1. *(a)* The term "B picture" refers to films that were made quickly on small budgets during the studio era and were often made to appear as the second movie in a double feature, to accompany the more expensive "A picture."

   (b) Manifest Destiny refers to a theory developed and popularized in the 19th century to provide a rationale for the United States to expand from the Atlantic Ocean to the Pacific Ocean.

   (c) *Stagecoach* is an important Western film directed by John Ford in 1939. The film was a commercially successful A picture and therefore conferred new importance on the Western. It also made a star out of John Wayne.

   (d) A genre is a category of works which are widely recognized as having similar plots, settings, themes, characters, and artistic styles.

   (e) Sam Peckinpah directed several important revisionist Westerns such as *The Wild Bunch* and *Pat Garrett and Billy the Kid*.

   (f) Monument Valley, a landscape full of unusually shaped buttes and red clay located in northern Arizona, was used as a location for many important Westerns, including *Stagecoach* and *The Searchers*, both directed by John Ford. Ford used the valley often, and is often associated with it.

   (g) A myth is a story a culture tells about itself to explain its relationship to the world at large and to define the individuals that comprise it.

   (h) Spaghetti Westerns is a term used to describe Italian Westerns made in the 1960s and 1970s.

2. *(b)* is false.

3. Here is one way of answering the question: Native Americans have tended to be depicted as violent savages, embodiments of the chaotic forces of nature, which the white settlers are attempting to tame. Often, Westerns use white culture to represent civilization, progress, learning, and positive values, while Native Americans represent savagery, primitivism, mindless violence, and inhumanity. Since the Western presents the conflict between nature and culture, white people—by setting up Native Americans as being nearly inhuman—have chosen to represent themselves as culture and Native Americans as nature; this is unfair be-

cause Native Americans themselves have always had a culture. It is also worth noting that Hollywood has not given Native Americans the opportunity to represent and define themselves onscreen.

4. *(a)* true; *(b)* false; *(c)* true; *(d)* true.

5. Your essay could take several points of departure, depending on your point of view. If you agree with Schatz that the Western is about loss and regret, you might begin by citing some of the key Westerns in which this theme is prominent, such as *The Man Who Shot Liberty Valance, Shane, Fort Apache, The Big Sky, The Outlaw Josey Wales,* and others. You could then go on to argue that this sense of loss is implicit in any Western, since the conflict between culture and nature on which the genre is based necessarily ends with the partial destruction of nature. A certain kind of civilization is gained in the Western, but it is gained at the expense of innocence and the total freedom afforded by a lawless, wide-open landscape. If you disagree with Schatz, you might begin by noting that although some Westerns are about loss and regret, these emotional states are the result of particular directors' visions of the West and are not necessarily built into the genre. For example, a television series like "Bonanza" is obviously part of the genre, yet the saga of the Cartwrights appears to have little to do with loss; instead it is mainly about financial gain, confidence in civilization, and the struggle against lawlessness, with little regret shown for the loss of the wilderness the Cartwrights have claimed as their personal property.

UNIT 5:

1. You were asked to write about your favorite music video—something you were already familiar with. Now, when judging your work, take a step back and imagine that you knew nothing about the video before you read your response. Have you brought the video to life for your reader? Are your descriptions clear and colorful? Even in rough form your notes should be descriptive and accurate.

2. If you had any trouble finding out who directed the video online, you may want to ask a librarian to help you with internet research, which will be increasingly necessary for any research project you do in this course or any course you take in the future. In any case, judge your work using the criteria immediately above—clarity, accuracy, color—but be a little more self-critical. In other words, read your work as though you were your own professor.

3. How detailed is your treatment? How descriptive is it? A good way of answering these questions is to show the treatment to a friend or family

member and see how he or she responds to it. In any case, ask yourself the following questions: Does the treatment conform to audience expectations in the way it looks? (Examples: Does your country-western video take place in a rural or an urban setting? Does your alternative music video feature a cast of unknowns or have you cast an Oscar-winning movie star?) Examine the way you have illustrated the music with images? Have you decided to tell a story? If so, is the story clear? Have you done away with narrative? If so, what is your video about? *Why* have you made the artistic choices you have made?

ANSWERS TO SELF TEST

1. (a) *Chicago* is the Oscar-winning 2002 musical.
   (b) Trey Parker is the creator, with Matt Stone, of *South Park: Bigger, Longer & Uncut.*
   (c) The dancer-choreographer Gene Kelly appeared in *Singin' in the Rain* and other musicals.
   (d) *Ekstasis* is a Greek word, meaning "standing outside of oneself," used to describe the sense of pleasurable displacement that is key to the musical as a genre.
   (e) Queen Latifah is one of the stars of *Chicago.*
   (f) Busby Berkeley, the great choreographer, transformed backstage musical spaces into transcendental fantasy spaces.
   (g) Judy Garland was the star of *The Wizard of Oz* and other musicals.
   (h) Arthur Freed is the producer credited with developing the fully-integrated musical.

2. (a), (b), (c), and (d) are false.

3. The term *lift* refers to the sudden movement up from, out of, and away from the laws that govern the more everyday world of the narrative whenever a musical sequence begins—the experience of ecstasy enjoyed by singing, dancing characters and, it is hoped, the audiences who watch them.

4. (a) true; (b) false; (c) false; (d) false.

5. Judge your essay first by looking up the definition of any terms you used in the glossaries of *American Cinema/American Culture* and this study guide. Then evaluate the content of your essay by asking a friend or family member to read it and discuss it with you. Was your reader convinced that you knew what you were writing about? If the reader was familiar with the music video you discussed, did he or she learn anything new from your essay? If the reader had not seen the music video, did he or she find your description and interpretation clear? As

always, it's not your opinions that make an essay good; it's the quality with which you express them.

UNIT 6:

1. Although the content of the exercise will be very different, use the answer key in Unit 4, Exercise 2, as a means of judging your work. Here, you may discover that comedy is more a matter of how a given scene is treated than what the scene actually contains. In other words, both of your scenes may contain threats of violence, and yet the *context* in which those threats occur, the specific ways in which the threats are voiced and acted upon, will spell the difference between, say, histrionic melodrama and raucous comedy.

2. The issue of film censorship is so contentious and long-standing that your problem here will have been to trim the subject to a manageable length. However you respond to the issue in terms of your personal opinions, you must nevertheless judge your essay on the basis of its contents, not its point of view. In broad terms, you ought to have defined each of the current ratings categories, noted the name of the organization that issues the ratings, and cited at least one specific film's rating as a case in point. If you pursued the issue of sociological studies about sex and violence in the movies, you should have noted specifically who issued the study, described clearly what the study found, and used the data as points of argument. Finally, your essay should contain a coherent and well-developed thesis at the beginning and a sharp conclusion at the end.

3. See Supplementary Unit B for a sample close analysis.

4. Judge your essay on its depth and detail. If you agreed with the theorist, how well did you spell out his theory? Do the examples you chose from films *really* support the theory, or did you tailor them to fit your essay? If you argued with the theorist, did you describe his theory fairly and accurately? Do the examples you chose provide a genuine counterargument? How do you imagine they would respond to your arguments?

ANSWERS TO SELF TEST

1. (a) The Tramp is the antiauthoritarian hobo character Charles Chaplin portrayed in most of his films, including *The Circus, City Lights,* and *Modern Times.*

   (b) *Vulgus* is a Latin word meaning "the common people."

   (c) The democratizing function of American comedies is a concept describing the way romantic comedies sometimes resolve class conflicts in an idealized manner by way of marriages between men and women of different classes, as well as the theme of social integration often found in comedies about the immigrant experience.

   (d) Frank Capra directed *It Happened One Night,* the first screwball comedy.

   (e) The Production Code is a set of rules governing the content of Hollywood films, instituted in the early 1930s and made enforceable and more restrictive in 1934.

   (f) A screwball comedy is a type of romantic comedy, made mostly between 1934 and 1942, featuring an unusual amount of hostility between characters who are supposed to be in love.

   (g) *The Lady Eve* is a classic screwball comedy directed by Preston Sturges, starring Henry Fonda as a wealthy snake expert and Barbara Stanwyck as a con artist.

   (h) Sigmund Freud, the founder of psychoanalysis, thought that jokes worked as a form of emotional liberation.

2. (a), (b), and (d) are false.

3. Buster Keaton was a great silent comedian of the 1910s and 1920s who embraced the modern world with all its speed, machinery, and absurdism. Keaton's characters tend to be middle-class men who rely on common sense and know-how. His films include *Steamboat Bill, Jr., Sherlock Jr., The Cameraman, The General,* and *Seven Chances.*

4. (a) true; (b) false; (c) true; (d) false.

5. As you should know, there is critical debate over the extent to which the Great Depression affected American comedy. Some critics see Hollywood bridging class differences in the screwball comedy, since some of them end in marriages between a member of the upper class and a member of the middle or working classes. Others see the Great Depression reflected more indirectly through the questioning of social institutions like marriage and the exposure of gender and sexual tensions underlying the culture. Still others find the genesis of screwball comedy in Hollywood's Production Code, not in the Great Depression. Judge your response on the basis of its complexity and thoroughness.

6. Extra Credit: Answers may vary.

UNIT 7:

1. You could approach this treatment in a wide variety of ways. Your opinion of the war is not the issue. Judge your treatments on how clearly you define your characters, how well you convey the complexity of your story, and how thoroughly you conceive and convey significant details. For example, some possible characters might be: two young women, an African-American from Detroit, and a Jew from Berkeley, under the command of a hard-bitten career sergeant from Mississippi. Or, three guys separated from their platoon because of a jeep accident—two football players from Southern Methodist University and a library science student from a small college in Vermont. Or, you could go for Hollywood iconography—a Clint Eastwood type, a Charlie Sheen type, and a Jodie Foster type stuck together in the desert having arguments about politics, sexism, and baseball. For the Iraqis, two computer science students might find themselves in the middle of the desert led by a fanatic career officer willing to sacrifice his men to protect Saddam Hussein; or all three Iraqis could be dissidents struggling against the odds to remain alive in the face of a political system they despise. Whoever they are, all of your characters should be in situations that *challenge* them, and there should be some conflict *within* the American group at least and, preferably, within the Iraqi group as well. Your characters' experiences should *change* them in some significant way. Finally, read over your treatment and see if you can really *see* and *feel* the war.

2. Ask yourself what you learned from your interview subject. Did your subject tell you things you probably wouldn't find in history books? In addition, ask yourself how you might conduct such an interview differently in the future. Use the experience to learn something about your own ability to interact with others.

3. Your point of view on this question is not the issue; there are no right or wrong answers here. As with any exercise, judge your response on its logic and complexity. If you have trouble evaluating yourself, give your essay to a friend and ask for a second opinion. Ask that person if he or she is convinced by your argument. Find out how that person would have handled the assignment.

4. Evaluate your work on the basis of effort (how much work did you put into it?), depth (did you continually ask questions and get answers, or did you stop after the first round?), and learning (what do you know now that you did not know before?). If you wrote a paper on the subject, find a reader—a family member or a friend—who can be trusted to give you an honest assessment. The point is not simply to receive an evaluation of your work; sharing your knowledge with someone is important in itself.

ANSWERS TO SELF TEST

1. *(a)* The Office of War Information is the federal agency created during World War II to oversee American propaganda efforts.
   (b) "The ideal platoon" is a convention of the World War II combat film which set up an ethnically and racially mixed group of American heroes to represent a cross-section of the American people.
   (c) A newsreel is a short documentary film presenting news and current events.
   (d) *Apocalypse Now* is an important Vietnam war film directed by Francis Coppola.
   (e) Bataan is the site of an early World War II battle between the United States and Japan, and the subject of an early World War II combat film with that title.
   (f) Samuel Fuller is an American director who made a number of combat films about World War II and the Korean war.
   (g) Oliver Stone is the director of *Platoon* and *Alexander*.
   (h) Pacifism is an antiwar philosophy that seeks nonviolent solutions to conflict.

2. *(a)*, *(b)*, and *(c)* are false.

3. Combat films often have no female characters at all. They sometimes combine fictional sequences filmed entirely within the walls of a studio soundstage with actual newsreel footage of real battles. The "normal" world of the home-front is treated as an alien world, while the bizarre and deadly world of war becomes normal. They often center on communal group heroism rather than on the actions of an individual character.

4. *(a)* false; *(b)* false; *(c)* true; *(d)* false.

5. Your response should note many if not most of the following points: newsreels served as current events reporting of the war effort; they provided American audiences with motion pictures of important battles; they showed Americans what the war really looked like; they influenced Hollywood fiction films by revealing the physical reality of World War II; compared to newsreels, combat films made on studio back lots and in soundstages began to look artificial; newsreel footage of actual battles began to be inserted into fiction films to add to their sense of realism.

UNIT 8:

1. Here is a sample scene: The scene occurs between an aging actor and his young girlfriend, an aspiring actress. They are seated on the edge of a stage in a large, empty theater—the kind of place that comes to life when there are people in it but assumes a sad, lonely feeling after the show is over and everyone goes home. It's shabby, with faded upholstery on the seats and an old, dusty stage curtain that has been pulled closed. The theater is dark, except for two single work light bulbs hanging down on each side of the stage, creating deep shadows on the floor and walls and lighting both characters' faces with a mixture of harsh glare and deep darkness.

   The actor is wearing expensive sportswear, trying to look younger than he really is; the actress is wearing a cheap overcoat and a pair of running shoes. They are arguing about her career and his failure to live up to his promise of getting her a part in his hit play:

   > HER: "You're a pig."
   >
   > HIM: "I know."
   >
   > HER: "No, I don't think you do. You say, 'I know,' but that's just an act. Everything you do is an act."
   >
   > HIM: "That's who I am; you knew that when we met."
   >
   > HER: "And now I know I'm a fool."
   >
   > HIM: "But you're *my* fool. Let's go home."
   >
   > HER: "You just don't get it, do you? You're not going home. Ever." (She pulls out a gun and fires twice. He cries out. She laughs.) "Idiot—it's a stage gun full of blanks." (She turns to leave.) "I just wanted to see you cringe."

   The scene begins in a two shot, cutting to a close up of HER on the line, "No, I don't think you do." Cut to a medium shot of HIM on "That's who I am. . .," back to HER on her next line, and back to HIM on his line. The camera is on HER for the line, "You just don't get it, do you?", but cuts to a close-up of HIM for the rest of that line, recording a look of shock, fear, and horror. Cut to a close-up of a gun being fired, remaining on the gun as it smokes as we hear his cry. Cut back to a two shot for HER final line and exit.

2. *(a)* Orson Welles' *The Lady from Shanghai* begins as follows: As the credits roll, a high angle shot of water moves in waves toward the camera culminating in a single crashing wave. The image dissolves to a low angle shot of a bridge forming a striking diagonal composition on the screen; a tugboat passes under the bridge, moving from right to

left across the screen. It is dusk. Another dissolve leads to a shot of Central Park, with the New York City skyline in the background. As the dissolve occurs, a voice-over narrator says, "When I start to make a fool of myself, there's very little that can stop me."

The image of the park dissolves to a shot of the shadow of a carriage visible on the pavement in 3/4 angle. It is night. The camera tilts up as the carriage moves into the frame, then tracks with the carriage as it moves down the street, simultaneously tracking slowly forward on the woman riding in the carriage. As the dissolve occurs, the voice-over continues: "If I had known where it would end, I'd never let anything start—if I had been in my right mind, that is. But once I'd seen her—once I'd seen her—I was not in my right mind for a very long time." The image is very shadowy, except for the woman, who is brilliantly lit and whose image flickers to suggest, on a realistic level, passing street lamps. By the end of the shot, the woman's image nearly fills the frame.

3. When writing a paper on a topic such as this one, your primary tasks are to keep your research focused on a particular issue and avoid making broad generalizations on the basis of a few examples. In this case, judge your essay on its specificity: is your thesis statement manageable? Is the point arguable in a short paper? For example, "American women were happier during World War II because they could finally get jobs and earn money," is not a good thesis statement because it is imprecise (does the writer mean *all* American women worked and were happy during World War II?), and is not provable in a short paper. A more successful thesis statement would be, "Because many American men had to leave their jobs to serve in the armed forces during World War II, American women were given an unprecedented opportunity to enter the work force in jobs that had previously been limited to men."

4. Because there is a wealth of research material on McCarthyism and the Hollywood Ten, your task will have been to keep your topic narrow enough to handle in a short paper. Judge your response on the basis of its clarity and focus (see Example #3, above), and give yourself extra points for presenting different views of the era. If you discuss *Touch of Evil*, ask yourself how deeply you have gotten into the film. Have you talked about the way in which Welles films various scenes, or have you stayed on the level of plot descriptions?

ANSWERS TO SELF TEST

1. *(a)* Cinematography is photography for motion pictures.

   (b) German Expressionism was a stylistic movement in the cinema that tried to express psychological states in an external way through the use of distorted perspective, exaggerated camera angles, and dramatic lighting effects.

   (c) Deep focus is a technique in which objects and people in both the foreground and the background appear in equally sharp focus at the same time.

   (d) Joseph McCarthy was a United States senator who, in the late 1940s and early 1950s, led investigations into the extent that communism existed in the film industry.

   (e) Orson Welles was the director of the film *Citizen Kane*, a key influence on film noir. He also directed the noir film *The Lady from Shanghai*.

   (f) *Detour* is an important low-budget film noir about a man who becomes involved in an increasingly catastrophic chain of events involving murder and blackmail.

   (g) James M. Cain was a writer of so-called hard-boiled fiction. Two of his novels, *Double Indemnity* and *The Postman Always Rings Twice*, were made into noir films.

   (h) Realism in the cinema is difficult to define, but in the context of film noir it has to do with the documentary-like black-and-white cinematography, the use of real locations as settings, low-key lighting that creates a lot of shadows, and film noir's tendency to be about petty crimes and streetwise detectives, as opposed to flashy gangsters and gentlemen detectives. Film noir's realism was created in reaction against the glossy, supposedly unrealistic studio style of the 1930s.

2. *(c)* and *(d)* are false.

3. Martin Goldsmith is talking about Cain's use of strong, colorful language full of American vernacular, or slang. He is also describing the passionate emotions in Cain's novels—emotions found in film noir as well. In the program, Goldsmith cites the passage in Cain's novel *The Postman Always Rings Twice* in which a woman asks a man to bite her. These violent emotions can be seen in many film noirs, where men and women often find themselves committing crimes of passion.

4. *(a)* false; *(b)* false; *(c)* false; *(d)* true.

5. As with any essay question, there are many possible responses. You might have discussed any of the following issues: film as the expression of a director's worldview; film as the expression of wider cultural problems, such as changes in gender roles; the technical elements of film as

expressive devices; film noir as the expression of America's response to World War II and the nuclear threat; black and white cinematography reflecting a black-and-white moral scheme; and so on. You may have agreed with Bailey that film noir is, in fact, a matter of black and white, evil and good, or you may have disagreed and discussed the ways in which film noir is, both visually and morally, a matter of darkening shades of grey. Judge your answer on the basis of how many of these points—or others—you raised.

UNIT 9:

1. This is a fairly easy assignment, but if you have put some effort into it, it will reveal your own tastes and viewing patterns in a fresh way. Now that you have tabulated your film-going activities, do you think you are an average viewer? If not, why not? If so, how do you think your own tendencies as a consumer are reflected in the types of films that are made?

2. This is a primarily visual exercise, and there is no right or wrong way to do it. The goal of the assignment is to help you not only think about the aesthetic challenges widescreen processes offer to filmmakers but also *see* these challenges in a hands-on way. The sequence you design should clue you into the peculiarities of filming people in widescreen close-up, the challenges of maintaining spatial relationships between characters and objects, and the opportunities for creating complicated composi-tions with the added horizontal space. If you have been especially am-bitious, you will begin to see not only the challenges offered within in-dividual shots but also the difficulties of editing these shots together in seamless Hollywood style.

3. Dwight Macdonald provides a good deal of statistical information as well as quotations from sociologists and marketing experts to support his claims; your essay should include some of these specifics. In addi-tion, Macdonald rests his argument on social, psychological, cultural, and economic grounds, so you should have mentioned each of these ar-eas as well. Finally, Macdonald's position in regard to the burgeoning teen market is that of a skeptic. You might have agreed with him, or you might have taken issue with his position; in either case, you ought to have taken a position yourself. If you chose to compare the teen market of the 1950s with today's marketing environment, you should have bol-stered your claims with hard facts and detailed observations, rather than simply making broad claims based simply on your opinions. Though they are not irrelevant to a paper such as this, your opinions must be supported by evidence in order to be taken seriously.

4. Use as a guide the sample formal analysis found in Supplementary Unit B: "Thinking and Writing About Film." If you wish to pursue the subject of widescreen analysis further, read Charles Barr's essay, "CinemaScope: Before and After," noted in Section V of this unit: "Suggested Readings." Barr's theoretical position is well illustrated with practical examples from films; these examples will further clarify the aesthetic problems and benefits of CinemaScope and other widescreen processes.

ANSWERS TO SELF TEST

1. *(a)* An anamorphic lens "squeezes" a wide field of vision onto a piece of film in order to get a much wider image when projected.
   (b) *United States v. Paramount Pictures, Inc., et. al.* is the name of the legal case, decided by the Supreme Court, which broke the monopoly of the Hollywood studios by forcing them to give up control of their movie theaters.
   (c) Letterbox is the name given to videotape and DVD versions of widescreen films available in the correct aspect ratio.
   (d) The Production Code of Ethics is the list of topics that were considered unacceptable for Hollywood films beginning in the 1930s; the Code lost its authority in the 1950s.
   (e) Cinerama is a widescreen process involving a curved screen; it was developed in the 1950s.
   (f) 3-D gives the impression of depth to films by projecting two images on the screen and separating them visually by way of special glasses; as in normal vision, each eye sees a slightly different image, giving the appearance of depth.
   (g) Aspect ratio is the ratio of a film image's width to its height.
   (h) James Dean was a film star of the 1950s who came to represent rebelliousness, defiance, and disillusionment.

2. *(a)*, *(b)*, and *(d)* are false.

3. Unless they are shown on a particularly enlightened cable station, widescreen films are cropped to the shape of a television screen, resulting in a loss of image of between 20 and 48 percent. A process of "panning and scanning" creates false "camera movements" to cover important actions. This process often fails, however, with the result being scenes apparently occurring between two characters' noses, with the rest of their faces cut off by the sides of the screen.

4. *(a)* true; *(b)* false; *(c)* false; *(d)* true.

5. There is no right or wrong answer here; judge your response by its complexity. Did you think *visually*? Did you cite hypothetical examples? Here is a sample response:

All directors are bound by the technology of the medium, but there are important variations they can play with. One of these is the shape of the screen. Some directors are attracted to the widescreen image because it enables them to capture the horizontality of certain landscapes. Others use it because the wider screen provides the opportunity to film two people in close-up at the same time. In any event, widescreen processes provide a visual experience that cannot be duplicated at home, even with letterboxed images, because when widescreen films are exhibited in theaters they enhance the viewer's sensation of being surrounded by the image. Unfortunately, most Hollywood directors know that their films will eventually be shown on television, where the image will be cropped. As a result, some directors purposely avoid using the widest possible aspect ratios, while others tend to keep all important action in the middle of the image so that there will be less damage done when the film is cropped for television.

6. Extra credit: Digital Video Disc or Digital Versatile Disc.

UNIT 10:

1. You should have gone beyond the definitions of postmodernism offered in the textbook and the Study Guide, though these may of course play a role in your work. If you did cite other definitions, did you specify the sources of these definitions? If you produced a written essay, does the essay follow a coherent structure? Does it contain a clearly defined thesis statement? If you presented your work in the form of a scrapbook, how far did you go in selecting pictures and clippings? Ask yourself honestly: is there a wide variety of material here, or did I take the easiest possible route to completing the assignment? And did you notice any parallel between the topic of the scrapbook and the *nature* of the topic? In other words, is the scrapbook itself a pastiche?

2. The textbook tends to be rather more skeptical on the subject of postmodernism than the Study Guide, particularly in the sections dealing with the critique of postmodernism leveled by Fredric Jameson. Judge your work on the basis of its coherence and detail. For a guide to formal film analysis, use the sample close analysis offered in Supplementary Unit B: "Thinking and Writing About Film."

3. This is a fairly difficult assignment to the extent that it asks you to compare a foreign film to an American film without having been introduced

in class to the foreign cinema in question. Judge your work according to your ability to avoid generalizations! If you draw comparisons and contrasts between the French New Wave film and one or more Hollywood films, ask yourself whether you have really *proven* your familiarity with each. Note also that the French film will likely have been more confusing to you than any Hollywood film you have seen in this course. Some of the formal techniques employed by New Wave directors are designed to shake the viewer out of his or her routine view of the world and of the movies. Give yourself some points for attempting this assignment, and if you attempted to explain some of these disorienting film techniques, so much the better.

4. Literary and cultural theory is often written in a somewhat more technical language than you may be used to, and therefore it may be difficult at first to read and understand. However, you should have attempted to work through the difficulty to describe the critic's position clearly and fairly. If the critic is expressly political, how did you describe the politics? If you took issue with the critic, did you cite specific points and argue them? As always, judge your work on the basis of its coherence, the sophistication of your argument, and the level of detail you achieve. Note: this is an advanced assignment, perhaps more appropriate to an upper-level course than an introductory one. However, it has been included for those students who are able to tackle more difficult topics. Give yourself some extra points for attempting this assignment, and consider taking an advanced course in film or cultural studies to pursue these ideas further.

ANSWERS TO SELF TEST

1. *(a)* Postmodernism is a movement in art, music, literature, and film that rejects the principles of modernism by both appropriating and dismantling the conventions and styles of earlier eras.
   (b) Roger Corman was a very successful exploitation film producer and director, who gave many film school directors their first directing jobs.
   (c) Brian De Palma directed such films as *Sisters, Carrie, Obsession*, and others.
   (d) The French word for "author," *auteur* came to be used to describe a film director who achieved artistic control over his or her films.
   (e) *Taxi Driver* is a film by Martin Scorsese in which a deranged cab driver attempts to assassinate a politician but kills a pimp instead.
   (f) The French New Wave was a group of French film critics who admired certain Hollywood filmmakers and who became directors

themselves in the late 1950s and early 1960s; the group included Jean-Luc Godard, François Truffaut, Claude Chabrol, Eric Rohmer, and Jacques Rivette.

(g) The term pastiche means a work of art which is purposely jumbled in its construction—a hodgepodge of styles and references, with no apparent attitude toward the styles in question.

(h) Federic Jameson was the literary and cultural critic who described postmodernism in terms of nostalgia, "the failure of the new," and schizophrenia.

2. (b) and (d) are false.

3. Short answer: The time-travel motif found in such films as the *Back to the Future*, *Terminator*, and *Bill & Ted* series, as well as *Peggy Sue Got Married* and *Star Trek IV: The Voyage Home*, suggests a dissatisfaction with the present day and an attempt to alter the current situation by way of fantasies that rearrange the past or the future. This motif ties in with critic Fredric Jameson's argument that postmodernism is concerned with nostalgia because of a lack of identity and security in the present.

4. (a) false; (b) false; (c) false; (d) false.

5. Postmodernism is an artistic movement and cultural phenomenon that rebelled against modernism by rejecting principles of stylistic unity and coherence of expression in favor of pastiche, parody, and allusion for their own sake. In film history, postmodernism is reflected in the film school generation's nostalgic appropriation of older films' narratives and stylistic figures—in other words, references to previous films. Postmodernism is also reflected in certain movie brats' "incoherent texts"—films such as *Taxi Driver*, for example, with its fragmented narrative and contradictory central character.

UNIT 11:

1. Your review should include a thorough summary of the film's central ideas, a clearly stated thesis statement spelling out the argument you are going to make about the film's success or failure, and a point-by-point series of concrete examples of why you take the position you do. References to other programs in the course also help to ground your argument factually, but they are not required. Remember: regardless of whether you liked or disliked this film, you must move beyond a simple thumbs-up, thumbs-down description when reviewing it. Coming up with a cutting line is relatively easy; supporting it with evidence is more difficult.

2. New voices from the African-American, Latino, Asian-American, feminist, gay, lesbian, Greek, Native-American, Jewish, and many other communities are heard through independent filmmaking. They may be difficult to find, for distribution of independent films is often limited, but that is your task here. If you cannot find anything in newspapers or magazines, ask your librarian to help you locate reference books that could direct you to independent film distribution companies. If you are really ambitious, write to them and ask for their catalogues. Then try to convince your school to run an independent cinema night, with short films representing diverse points of view. Taking a hands-on role in independent American cinema may be the best lesson you could have.

3. The assignment is yours; make of it what you will. If your school does not have any magazines devoted to independent cinema, ask your librarian to consider subscribing to some.

4. See Supplementary Unit B: "Thinking and Writing About Film" for a sample close analysis.

ANSWERS TO SELF TEST

1. *(a)* The term guerilla filmmaking was coined by Spike Lee to describe the beg-borrow-and-steal methods used by independent filmmakers to finance, produce, direct, and distribute their work.

   (b) John Cassavetes, an American independent director, supported himself as an actor in Hollywood films and directed a number of independent feature films.

   (c) Splatter films is a term used to describe horror films (such as *Night of the Living Dead*) characterized by gory special effects.

   (d) Joel Coen directed such films as *Blood Simple*, *Barton Fink*, and *The Hudsucker Proxy*.

   (e) The first of several independent feature films made by John Sayles was *The Return of the Secaucus Seven*.

   (f) Zoetrope Studios, Francis Coppola's production company, was formed in an attempt to maintain Coppola's independence from the larger studios.

   (g) Robert Altman directed such films as *Nashville*, *McCabe and Mrs. Miller*, and *The Player*.

   (h) Divine was the 300-pound drag queen who starred in many of John Waters' films.

2. *(a)* and *(b)* are false.

3. The major difficulty is financing. There are too few funding sources for independent productions. In some other countries, many independent

features are produced for broadcast on television. Here, independent filmmakers rely on a piecemeal system of financing their films, so that directors may spend more time raising funds than they do actually making films.

4. *(a)* false; *(b)* true; *(c)* true; *(d)* false.

5. Your answer should include references not only to the independent visions of certain directors but also to the financial independence of their productions. You should have noted some of the independent directors mentioned in the Study Guide overview and interviewed in the program, and you might also have described some of these men and women in brief case studies concerning the difficulty of maintaining independence in the American cinema.

Glossary

A pictures During the 1930s and 1940s, when feature films were regularly shown as double features, the A picture was the more important, more expensive production featuring top stars, high production values, and (often, though not always) more carefully worked screenplays.

affect A psychological term used to describe an individual's emotional state or mental disposition.

allusion A reference, either implied or explicit, to a real person or place or to another work of art. An allusion in a film may serve to expand the meaning of the film by reminding viewers of the contents of another film.

aspect ratio The ratio of the image's width to its height. Various aspect ratios were used in silent cinema, but the most common was approximately 1.33:1. In 1932, the Academy of Motion Picture Arts and Sciences standardized the aspect ratio of Hollywood films to 1.33:1; this ratio became known as the Academy ratio or Academy aperture. In the 1950s, widescreen aspect ratios took the place of the Academy ratio. Some of these include 1.66:1 (European widescreen), 1.85:1 (American widescreen), 2.2:1 (70mm widescreen), and 2.35:1 (anamorphic projection).

axis/crossing the axis The axis is an imaginary line drawn through the physical space of a scene or sequence, separating the camera from the objects being filmed for the purpose of maintaining the objects' position and direction onscreen. If the camera crosses this axis at any point, the objects will appear to flip to the "wrong" side of the screen or, if the object is in motion, suddenly travel in the "wrong" direction. Imagine a shot of a man running from right to left onscreen; if the camera crosses the axis set up in this initial shot, subsequent shots would have the man running from left to right.

B pictures The cheaper, more quickly made film on the double bills of the 1930s and 1940s; the term "B picture" does *not* refer to a film's quality (B does not stand for "bad"), although their limited budgets and rapid production schedules often yielded results that were less than completely successful.

back lot The studio's backyard—the outdoor area, often quite vast, on which city blocks, village squares, and Western towns were built as sets for film productions—as well as its soundstages; as opposed to the "front offices," where the executives work.

blind bidding A common practice during the studio era in which exhibitors were forced to rent a film without having seen it, though they were provided with advance publicity materials.

block booking The practice of forcing exhibitors to rent films in groups rather than individually. For example, a film seen as being a likely hit would be paired with three potential bombs; in order to get the hit, the exhibitor would have to take the bombs. This was a standard practice during the studio era.

character actor Actors who tend to appear regularly *in secondary roles* as easily recognizable character types. (Note: the term "character actor" does not refer to *stars* who tend to play the same type of character again and again.)

CinemaScope A widescreen process introduced in 1953 by 20th Century-Fox in which a special camera lens, called an anamorphic lens, squeezes a wide rectangular image to almost half its width to record it on standard-sized film; another lens on the projector expands the image back to its correct rectangular width on the screen. CinemaScope's aspect ratio is 2.35:1. In film criticism, CinemaScope, or simply Scope, is often used to describe *any* widescreen process with a comparable aspect ratio.

cinematography Photography for motion pictures and all the elements used to accomplish it, including film stock, lights, lenses, filters, and so on.

classical Hollywood style The formal and narrative techniques developed in American filmmaking in the 1910s and 1920s and employed regularly by Hollywood studios; one of the key elements of Hollywood narrative style is the centrality of a single character in pursuit of his or her goals; in general, the formal techniques of classical Hollywood style are designed to enhance a feeling of identification between the audience and the central character.

close-up A shot taken (or appearing to be taken) from a position very close to the subject, isolating the subject or even part of the subject on the screen so that very little else is visible. A close-up of a face, for instance, leaves little room onscreen for any background; an extreme close-up of a single eye would fill the screen with just the eye and the facial area immediately around it.

composition The graphic arrangement of objects and people within the image. (In considering the idea of composition, think about the objects and people onscreen not in terms of their identity but rather their shape.)

convention An often-repeated element in any artistic medium that serves to telegraph a set of meanings and associations to an audience. For example, film conventions include barroom brawls in Westerns and shadowy old gothic houses in horror films. A contemporary convention is the montage sequence with background rock music inserted in a film to serve double use as a music video.

craning shot or crane A shot in which the camera itself is able to move up and down by way of a cherry picker or crane, allowing for extraordinary mobility and scope.

crosscutting A category of editing in which two scenes occurring simultaneously but in two different places are edited together, often for the purpose of heightening suspense.

cut The most common transition between shots, effected by physically cutting one shot to its desired length and splicing it with tape to another shot.

deconstruction A term originated in literary theory to describe the act of analytically dismantling a given object—a book, a poem, a film—not only to see its component ideological parts but also to undermine the security and fixedness of any meaning that appears to arise from it.

deep focus A technique in which objects in both the immediate foreground and distant background of the image appear in equally sharp focus.

demographic Relating to the statistical breakdown of a population into various segments by race, age, sex, religion, and so on.

digital recording A system of sound recording in which sounds are converted into a series of binary numbers so that when they are played back by way of a computer, which stores the numbers and converts them back into sounds, any surface noise from the recording medium will be eliminated.

dissolve A transition between shots in which the first shot slowly fades out as the second shot fades in, creating a superimposition in the middle of the transition when both shots are midway between fading in and fading out.

Dolby system A patented noise-reduction system that produces greater fidelity by electronically boosting the recorded sound during playback as a way of overcoming background noise.

dolly See *tracking shot*.

DVD Digital Video Disc, or Digital Versatile Disc. The size of a CD, or compact disc, a DVD can store well over two hours of high-quality digital video and up to eight tracks of CD-quality digital audio.

eye-level shot A shot taken at the level of an average adult human being's vision, namely 5 to 6 feet from the ground.

eye-line matches A type of matching in which continuity between shots is maintained through the direction of characters' lines of vision. In this way, individual characters in separate shots appear to look at each other.

fade-in A transition in which the image gradually emerges from either pitch darkness or bright whiteness, assuming increasing definition along the way.

fade-out The opposite of a fade-in; the image slowly loses its definition as it makes the transition to complete black or white.

frame One of the individual pictures seen on a strip of developed motion picture film. In sound film, there are 24 frames for every second of running time. The term also refers to the rectangular shape of the projected image.

genre In any art form, a category of works which are widely recognized as having similar plots, settings, themes, characters, and artistic styles. In film, a genre is a group of films which are linked together by common narrative conventions and recognized as such by audiences. Some popular genres are the Western, the horror film, the musical, and the combat film.

German Expressionism A stylistic movement in the cinema that sought to render interior psychological states in an external way through the use of distorted perspective, exaggerated camera angles, dramatic lighting effects, and so on; the cinematic movement was itself an outgrowth of earlier trends in painting, theater, literature, and architecture.

graphic matches Matches made according to the shapes and positions of the objects being filmed; for instance, a common effect of graphic matching is that characters in conversation with each other tend to remain in the same positions onscreen from shot to shot instead of flipping back and forth.

high-angle shot A shot taken from above the subject, looking down.

high-key lighting In the three-point lighting system used in classical Hollywood style, the "key light" is the chief light source, the "fill light" is the weaker light sources that fill in shadows cast by the key light, and the "back light" illuminates the space behind the characters in order to distinguish them from the background; high-key lighting thus refers to a high ratio of fill lights to the key light, thereby washing out any shadows cast by the key light and creating a more or less brightly and uniformly lit scene. See *low-key lighting*.

identification The experience, often less than fully conscious, of placing oneself in the role of a film character or, in the case of a star, of closely relating one's own feelings and characteristics to the imagined feelings and observable characteristics of the star.

independent cinema Films made outside of the traditional studio system and/or by independent producers (such as David O. Selznick, Samuel Goldwyn, or Walter Wanger) within it. Contemporary independent cinema is generally financed independently—that is, without funding from and before having a contract with a major distributor. Even the most radical, unusual, or controversial film cannot be considered "independent" if it is financed by a major studio.

integrated musical A musical that ties the songs and dance numbers into the world of the story, as opposed to a musical revue—a series of vaudeville-like acts strung together without regard for how their content relates from number to number.

isolationism A political philosophy that seeks to limit American involvement in world affairs.

jump cut A type of editing designed to create a sudden "jump" in time or space. For instance, if a single shot of a character walking slowly across the screen was edited into three separate shots by eliminating some of the footage, the character would appear to hop jerkily across the screen.

lighting The way in which light, natural or artificial, models people and objects within the image.

long shot A shot taken (or appearing to be taken) from a great distance from the subject, showing the subject in its entirety, along with some of the surrounding landscape or environment.

low-angle shot A shot taken from below the subject, looking up.

low-key lighting A lighting style in which the ratio of fill lights to the key light is low, thereby creating a shadowy, uneven distribution of light. See *high-key lighting* for definitions of "fill light" and "key light."

major studios, or "majors" The five biggest studios during the studio era (M-G-M, Paramount, Warner Bros., 20th Century-Fox, and RKO), the majors owned extensive theater chains as well as production facilities and distribution networks.

Manifest Destiny A term introduced in 1845 to suggest the seeming inevitability of the United States's territorial expansion into Texas; the term remained in use throughout the 19th century and came to refer to expansion into the Oregon territories, the Southwest, Hawaii, Alaska, and even the Philippines.

mass production The manufacturing of goods in large numbers, generally using machinery and a specialized labor force.

master shot A shot that is *(a)* taken from a position from which the entire field of action is visible and *(b)* taken continuously, without interruption, into which medium shots and close-ups may be intercut later.

matching on action A type of matching in which a character's or object's motion is used to create a visual bridge between shots. For example, a baseball tossed out of the image in shot A flies into the image in shot B.

medium shot A shot taken (or appearing to be taken) from mid-distance, showing for example a character or group of characters from the knees or waist up.

minor studios, or "minors" The three most important (Columbia, Universal, and United Artists) of the smaller, less heavily capitalized companies during the studio era; they were "minor" because they did not own their own theaters.

mise-en-scene All of the elements that produce expressive meaning in the image, including the setting, the lighting, the distance between the subject and the camera, and so on.

modernism A broad twentieth-century movement in the arts which attempted to respond to an increasingly technological and chaotic world by various formal techniques, depending on the art in question. Literary modernists like James Joyce employed multiple points of view in a single work as well as stream-of-consciousness narration. Modernist painters like Picasso and Braque depicted a single subject from multiple perspectives. And modernist architects such as Mies Van Der Rohe tried to strip architecture of any applied decoration, instead creating buildings in which "form followed function," thus revealing the spare technical elegance of seemingly simple materials like steel and glass.

monopoly One company's exclusive or near-exclusive ownership of a given industry or product offered for sale, thereby making fair competition impossible.

montage Another word for editing. In the United States, the word montage is usually used to describe sequences with short shots and rapid transitions—often dissolves, superimpositions, and jump cuts. For example, a film about an aspiring actress might contain a career montage composed of shots of the actress taking singing lessons, working out in a gym, running to auditions, and taking bows after a performance, all in 30 seconds.

myth The story or set of stories a culture tells about itself to explain its relationship to the world at large and to define the individuals that comprise it. In ancient Greek society, even when people stopped believing in the actual existence of the Olympian gods, they may still have believed in the *myths* of the gods because these myths explained aspects of Greek culture. Similarly, one does not have to believe that working cowboys are depicted realistically in the movies to appreciate the cowboy as myth.

newsreel Short documentary or documentary-style films presenting news and current events. Usually, newsreels were composed of footage of actual events, but sometimes supposedly real events were reenacted with actors. Until television news took their place in the 1950s, newsreels provided American cinema audiences with moving pictures of important world events, yet they were generally presented as entertainment rather than as objective news analyses. Newsreels were usually screened in theaters before the feature film.

Office of War Information A federal agency created during World War II to oversee American propaganda efforts. The OWI monitored Hollywood scripts and influenced story development as a way of promoting positive images of the United States and more informed (though unswervingly negative) views of the Axis powers.

oligopoly The exclusive or near-exclusive ownership of a given industry by several companies acting in concert; in other words, a group monopoly.

Other A theoretical concept of how human beings define and relate to one another. Instead of defining one's relationship to other people as "me vs. them," the theory of Otherness defines this relationship as "me vs. *not* me." The Other thus becomes defined by all the unspoken fears and desires one has about oneself. In the World War II combat film, the Japanese are seen as the Other; characterizations of the Japanese in these films say more about American fears than they say about what Japanese people are really like. In the Western, Native Americans are the Other; they tend to represent everything white people are supposedly not: uncivilized, childlike, primitive, and sexually threatening.

pacifism An antiwar philosophy that seeks nonviolent solutions to conflict.

pan The result of a horizontal rotation of the camera on a fixed base; in other words, the camera swivels from left to right or right to left but does not move from its fixed place on the ground.

Panavision Any of a series of widescreen processes developed by the company of that name. Some are anamorphic processes (see CinemaScope, above), but some use unsqueezed images on 70mm prints. Panavision aspect ratios range from 2.2:1 to 2.7:1. Note: Panavision, Inc., makes several types of film cameras, so when a given film cites the use of Panavision lenses in the end credits, it does not necessarily mean that the film is in Panavision.

parallel action Another term for crosscutting.

parody An artistic mode in which the qualities of a given, usually well-known work or genre are satirically mimicked and ridiculed; often, parody functions as a critique of the subject being parodied, exposing its flaws and weak points.

pastiche A work of art in any form (painting, literature, dance, music, and so on) which is purposely jumbled in its construction—a hodgepodge of styles and references. For example, a musical pastiche might begin with an imitation of Bach, slide into Count Basie, abruptly shift to Balinese gamelan, and end up like the Rolling Stones.

persona From the term used to describe the masks worn in ancient Greek theater, the constructed identity of an actor or star. An actor's persona is constructed from the roles he or she plays; a star's persona is constructed additionally from his or her appearances in the news, in ads, and in other cultural products outside of films.

phenomenology The philosophy that underlies the branch of film criticism that emphasizes the creative experience of watching films—as opposed to *materialist* criticism, which studies the cinema as the product of particular economic, linguistic, and cultural systems, or *formalist* film criticism, which tends to be more interested in a film's style rather than its content (or, better, which sees a film's style *to be* its primary content).

point of view shot A shot which purports to show precisely what a character sees, though of course it is only an approximation, since a camera lens does not "see" in the same way that human eyes do. Sometimes, point-of-view shots are signaled by masking, as when a character is seen lifting a pair of binoculars to his or her eyes, and the following point-of-view shot is masked to form two overlapping circles of vision.

postmodernism An artistic movement chronologically following modernism in which historical styles and figures are used in a playful, satirical, often purely decorative manner, thereby stripping them of their original context, meaning, and purpose.

poverty row A term used to describe a group of small film companies in Hollywood during the studio era. The most successful of these was Columbia; others were Monogram and Republic.

Production Code The set of guidelines adopted by the Motion Picture Producers and Distributors of America that governed the contents of Hollywood films in terms of on-screen depictions of and references to sex, violence, drugs, religion, abortion, and marriage. The Production Code was adopted in 1930; it became enforceable in 1934 when the Production Code Administration was established.

proscenium arch Literally, the wide opening on a stage separating the space on which the drama is played from the audience's space. Figuratively, the term is used to refer to the difference in theater between fiction (the events played on stage) and reality (the audience in their seats). In film, this distinction is blurred. There is no architectural element, such as an archway, to keep the audience separated from the characters, and in fact the camera is able move into the characters' space freely and smoothly.

schlock A slang term used to describe low-budget films about trashy or seemingly trashy subjects. Cheap horror films and teen pictures are often called schlock. Examples of schlock include, but are not limited to, such films as *Teenage Zombies, Juvenile Jungle, Daughter of Dr. Jekyll,* and *Flight Time Stewardesses.*

screwball comedy A type of romantic comedy featuring an unusual amount of hostility between characters who are otherwise supposed to be in love. Most classic screwball comedies were made between 1934 and 1942, though they appeared as late as 1952.

serials A series of feature films about the exploits of the same central character or characters and marketed as such; Western serials were popular in the 1930s; the James Bond films are a kind of contemporary serial, as are the Freddie Krueger and Jason films.

shot A piece of motion picture film that has been exposed in a camera in a single, uninterrupted run. The shot is the basic element of filmmaking, a sort of building block from which whole films are built.

soundstage A barnlike but acoustically sophisticated structure built for shooting films; a good soundstage must be high enough to accommodate crane shots, wide enough for crowd scenes, and capable of carrying the enormous electrical load demanded by elaborate film lighting equipment.

splatter films Films, usually in the horror genre, which contain explicit and protracted violence depicted by way of graphic special effects, especially gushing stage blood and fake human entrails (e.g., *Night of the Living Dead*).

steadicam A patented device that fits around a camera operator's waist and eliminates the inadvertent bumps and jerks that otherwise occur with hand-held cameras, allowing the operator to walk, run, or maneuver through rocky ground without disrupting the smooth movement of the shot.

stereophonic sound Sound recorded separately on two or more tracks and played back through two or more speakers. Dolby Stereo is currently the most popular patented stereophonic process for film recording and exhibition. The effect is a particularly clear sound quality with great range and fidelity, with different areas of the screen appearing to serve as the sound's source. For example, the sound of a car speeding across the screen will fade in and out of different speakers *behind* the screen to give audiences the impression that the sound itself is "moving."

storyboard A sequential series of drawings—rather like a comic strip—representing individual shots, or parts of shots, planned for a film. Storyboards help filmmakers design setups, camera movements, and editing patterns well in advance of the actual filming.

surround sound An effect produced in many movie theaters—and increasingly, but less spectacularly, in home entertainment units—by which sounds recorded on a separate track are played back through speakers at the sides and rear of the theater or living room. The effect attempts to place the audience *aurally* within the film, with sound coming from all sides.

three-shot A medium shot or medium close-up of three people.

tilt A vertical rotation of the camera on a fixed base; in other words, the camera looks up and down but does not itself rise or fall from its position on the ground.

tracking shot or track A shot in which the camera moves physically from one place to another on the ground. Sometimes, the camera moves on railroadlike track; other times it moves on wheels. The term can be further modified by direction, as in "forward tracking shot" or "lateral tracking shot."

transition The way in which one shot is attached to another shot; some types of transitions are: cut, dissolve, fade-in, and fade-out (see individual definitions of these terms).

treatment An early version of a screenplay, usually written in prose form in the present tense, that describes the central characters, important settings, and crucial plot points of the film.

two-shot A medium shot or medium close-up of two people.

vertical integration An industrial structure in which several different levels of production and marketing are tied together in corporate unity; in the case of the studio system, the term refers to the studios' control not only of the production of films but also their distribution and exhibition.

VistaVision A widescreen process developed by Paramount Pictures to compete with CinemaScope. In VistaVision, 35mm film was run through the camera *horizontally* rather than vertically, thereby enabling a wider image to be filmed. To be at their best in terms of image quality, VistaVision films had to have their own horizontally configured projectors, but most theater owners refused to install the special equipment.

wipe A transition, created by laboratory processing, in which one shot replaces another shot onscreen in a windshield wiper effect, with the first shot on one side of the wiper and the following shot on the other side.

Wipes can take many forms: star wipes, spiral wipes, vertical wipes, horizontal wipes, iris wipes, and so on.

zoom shot or zoom A shot taken with a lens with a variable focal length, shifting between wide-angle and long-focus or telephoto. Zooming may yield an impression of camera movement, even though the camera remains in a fixed position. (Note: the terms *zooming* and *tracking* cannot be used interchangeably. See *tracking shot*, above.) Aesthetically, zooms may express a shift in subjective awareness or consciousness. For example, if a character is searching for a friend in a crowd, a zoom shot of the friend could indicate a change in the character's consciousness—the zoom tells the audience that the character has located his or her friend in the crowd.